EN ROUTE TO MOOSEHEART—The family of the late Paul Van Zenten of Sharon, Pa., is shown as they arrived at the Dearborn station in Chicago on their way to Mooseheart to make their new home. Pictured with their luggage (left to right) standing are Paul, 13; Jeanette, 9; Mrs. Dorothy Van Zenten, the mother, and Virginia, 16; seated, William, 12; Robert, 9; Jack, 8, and Warren 5. Mooseheart is the home and school for dependent children of deceased members owned and operated by the Loyal Order of Moose.

THE
RED CABOOSE

an Orphan's Journey

JEANETTE VAN ZANTEN STUMP

The Red Caboose-An Orphan's Journey
© 2016 Jeanette Van Zanten-Stump

www.redcaboose.biz

Print ISBN: 978-1-54392-365-0
eBook ISBN: 978-1-54392-366-7

Dedicated to:

Dr. Raymond Francis, for your guidance, support
and encouragement.

A Note from the Author

●────────────────●

*T*he *Red Caboose-An Orphan's Journey* is a memoir of the ten years I lived at Mooseheart, an orphanage located thirty-eight miles west of Chicago, Illinois and the next ten years it took me to acclimate to life outside an institution in St. Mary's, Pennsylvania. My father died when I was three years old, and I lost my mother to mental illness leaving me parentless.

One definition of an orphan is bereft of parents. At Mooseheart, there were half-orphans and whole orphans. Some children had one living parent and often fared better than the children who lost both of their parents in death. For those of us who's mothers were alive, the majority of our moms also lived at Mooseheart, and we had at least one person who would go to bat for us, the best they could. I respect and admire the whole orphans who survived the ordeal without any parents.

Mooseheart was started by the Moose Club as a haven to help children who's fathers fought in World War I and lost their lives. In 1913, James J. Davis opened the doors of Mooseheart the Child City and School of the thousand-acre campus.

The Moose Club is a fraternal and service organization that James J. Davis salvaged in 1903. He increased the defunct membership of the

Moose from two lodges and a mere 246 members-he was the 247th- to over 1700 lodges and 600,000 members during his reign as director general.

According to Chester Harris, author of *Tiger at The Bar-The Life story of Charles J. Margiotti*, Davis received the initiation fees of each member that made him a millionaire. Support from fellow Moose members helped him obtain status as a senator of Pennsylvania.

In the early 1930's Davis was accused of money laundering over a million and a half dollars through lotteries, using Mooseheart as a ruse to get members to buy tickets. Moose Clubs received a third of the money and Mooseheart-a paltry ten percent of the lottery winnings. The remainder of the money lined the pockets of Davis and three other Moose members.

The Moose Club wasn't alone in it's lottery scheme; the Eagles, the Shriners and the Knights of Columbus were also indicted for similiar crimes. I find it sad that a few greedy people use well-meaning organizations for their own profit.

Marigotti, Davis' attorney, was able to pull at the heartstrings of the jury by using the testimony of four Mooseheart grads and a map of the miniature town of Mooseheart. Unlike orphanges such as St. Josephs in Erie, Pennsylvania located on a crowded downtown block, Mooseheart had a spread of over a thousand acres with two hundred separate buildings that housed 13,000 orphans with it's own water, sewage and street systems, hospital, schools and workshops. The ploy worked and the jury found Davis innocent.

Despite the acquittal, Davis' wasn't able to shake free of a nickname given to him by Governor Gifford Pinchot. He went to the grave being called "The man who milked the Moose."

While I was at Mooseheart, one of the things I detested most was being a poster child for the Moose Organization. On holidays and at different times throughout the year, matrons dressed us up in our Sunday clothes for a photo to be splashed on the front of the monthly Moose Magazine.

My picture appeared at least twice on front of the Moose Magazine; my first day of first grade and a picture of me and a couple of other children sitting on top of a life size stuffed moose with real antlers and fur, named Morgan the Moose. The moose was chosen as a mascot for the Moose Club because the strong, protective male animal takes care of it's own. My mom had a collection of glossy black and white 8 X 10 photos of my siblings and me, that were sent back to the Sharon Moose lodge in hopes of extra donations.

As much as I hated having my picture taken to elicit money from Moose members, I felt worse for a little boy named Percy who was in my grade. Although Percy had natural curly hair, he was taken to the beauty shop to have his hair curled so he looked like the picture of a little boy kneeling in front of the clock tower saying his prayers. This picture is displayed in Moose Clubs. Percy was then paraded around Moose Clubs in his pajamas to pull at the heart strings of Moose members, in hopes of donations.

Even now, at every Moose Club across the country at 9:00 p.m., chimes ring and a prayer is said for the children at Mooseheart with eyes focused on the little boy saying his prayers. Afterwards, a donation basket is passed around the bar. The majority of Moose Members, who support Mooseheart by donating money and goods, are good-hearted people who want to help children and to them I give thanks.

To this day, I refuse to give or to raise money for charitable organizations, because I'm skeptical where the money is actually going. Also, I don't have to feel like a needy orphan when I ask for money. I try to help people directly as much as possible and by the grace of God, haven't been in a situation where I needed charity.

Not everyone experienced Mooseheart the same way that I did. Some alumni have fond recollections and refer to it as their home, refusing to call it an orphanage. Some children were compliant and obeyed the rules. But there were also children, like me, who balked at the rigid, insti-tutionalized life.

What we have in common is that we all are grateful we had a roof over our head, food on the table and clothes to wear. But there is more to raising a child than caring for their physical needs. I don't know one per-son who lived at Mooseheart that can say their emotional needs were met through love and nurturing.

One question we probably all ask ourselves is "where would we have been without Mooseheart?" I don't have an answer and I'll never know. But I have talked to people who were orphaned, some who almost went to Mooseheart but didn't because extended family cared of them; they are functioning members of society.

When people ask what life was like at Mooseheart, I tell them that I had a good education, a roof over my head, food on the table and was instilled with a strong work ethic. When they ask if I was treated well, I tell them my truth, which I am now telling you. Unfortunately, Mooseheart isn't only a haven for children, but it's also a haven for child predators. Child abuse clearances were unheard of in the 1960's when I was there- not that they make a difference. As late as 2009, child sexual abuse at Mooseheart was reported in the Aurora Beacon News. Sadly, the Moose Club doesn't always protect it's own, especially the young and vulnerable. https://www.highbeam.com/doc/1G1-87475427.html

Although the majority of names are real, I've included a few fictitious names to protect people's privacy. When I started sharing this book with my brother Jack, he questioned about whether things happened exactly as I was writing them. I reminded him that my writings, especially the first three years of my life, were perceived through the eyes of a child. I researched events and pieced together what may or may not have happened.

The Red Caboose-An Orphan's Journey is Creative Non-Fiction. For anyone who is offended by what I wrote about them, I will use a quote from the writer Anne Lamont, "You own everything that happened to you. Tell your stories. If people wanted you to write warmly about them, they should have behaved better."

It's taken me nearly two decades, as many years as I was confined and the years it took for me to acclimate to life outside of an orphanage, to write this book. When I first decided to write my story, I couldn't have imagined the physical, emotional and spiritual toll on my life. I've gone years without writing a word because I needed to care for myself and family first.

Long before I began writing this memoir, I came across a saying that I cross stitched and is hanging on my kitchen wall. "Life can only be understood backwards, but it must be lived forwards." Soren Kierkegaard.

The day you were born, a ladder was set up to help you escape from this world.

—Rumi

Prologue 2012

———•———•———

I t was a cold rainy day with clouds hanging over the city of Pittsburgh when I pulled into the parking lot of the Amtrack train station. The hands on the clock tower of the red brick depot read 9:45; I was fifteen minutes late. When all of the black, plastic molded seats in the waiting room of the station were empty, my heart dropped.

My nine-year-old granddaughter and I had just traveled nearly three hours from Ridgway, Pennsylvania to pick up a childhood friend I hadn't seen in over forty years. Valerie and Lilly, her eight-year-old daughter, were scheduled to arrive from California.

My thoughts began to race. Perhaps Valerie got off the train in Chicago to visit her sister but didn't get back on. What possessed me to invite a person I hadn't seen or barely heard from in over forty years to come live with me? Valerie and I lived in an orphanage called Mooseheart together, from the time we were three years old until we were twelve years old. Mooseheart, The Child City and School, sponsored by Moose Clubs is an orphanage located thirty-eight miles west of Chicago.

Despite losing touch, I hadn't forgotten Valerie because I still had the 8th-grade school picture she sent me after she left the orphanage. The photo was tucked away in the drawer of my musical, wood jewelry box. In

2001, when the internet was in it's infancy I found an Alumni website for Moosheart, which had been in the far recesses of my mind.

I was sure in this day and age of foster care and government assistance to needy families the institution had closed by now. As I surfed the internet, I discovered Moosehart was still in operation and groveling for money to help the orphaned children. At the time, the organization was asking for millions of dollars to continue it's operating costs. Buried feelings of outrage surfaced to my psyche.

I couldn't believe that the Moose Club was still at it's antics of using children to raise money. I couldn't understand the outrageous operating costs. The Moose owned acres of prime land near the Chicago suburbs and the children weren't wearing designer clothes or driving BMW's. When my connection to the Moose came up in conversation with friends and community members, I didn't hesitate to vent my frustration.

Thankfully, the alumni website wasn't asking for donations to support the Moose or I wouldn't have used it. Valerie's older sister, June and I connected. When I emailed June, and asked about her younger sister Valerie, I was delighted when she gave me her California mailing address.

Valerie didn't have a computer, so we wrote handwritten letters back and forth. When she got a cell phone, we began calling each other. Valerie had two daughters; I had four children and five grandchildren. Valerie was a dental hygienist; I was a nutritionist. Both of us suffered from depression.

My thoughts continued to race. Maybe it's for the best; I don't know that much about her and people change over time. She could be a drug addict or a thief and wipe out my house and the little savings we have. After all, we got caught stealing soap from a dispensary and received detention. And we did try to smoke dried banana peels. Maybe she went on to heavier drugs.

As I was turning around to leave the station, I spotted a staircase with marble steps and a stainless-steel handrail. At the top of the steps was a woman exactly my age with bleach blonde hair and a nine-year-old little girl sleeping on a suitcase.

"Valerie!" I cried as I ran up the steps with my arms wide open to give her a hug.

She backed away from me and put her hand on her daughter's shoulder and started shaking her. "Lilly, wake up our ride is here." The young girl was dressed in skin tight black capris, a short sleeve white shirt with sparkles, sandals with thin straps. Her thick black hair was tangled from sleeping on the train. She stretched and rubbed her dark brown eyes, looking to see who was here to pick her up.

Valerie turned to me, "Sis; she said she would never get on another train again."

I hoped she would never have to. I hoped they would be happy in Pennsylvania and that Valerie would be able to find work, get a car, and an apartment in the beautiful little community of Ridgway. Valerie didn't introduce Lilly to me and didn't make eye contact long enough for me to introduce my granddaughter, Paige to her.

I helped haul the heavy luggage down the steps. Valerie slung a large black leather handbag over her left shoulder and carried a thick Frank Sinatra autobiography and some towels under her right arm.

When Valerie opened the passenger door of my silver Caravan mini-van, she pulled out a towel to put on the seat before she sat down. After getting into the van, she began rummaging through her purse and pulled out a cleaning rag and began wiping the door handles of the car door and the dash saying, "I brought plenty of old toothbrushes to clean with."

"Okayyyyyyy," I replied.

Images of eight and nine-year-old girls wearing night gowns flashed through my mind. My knees began to ache. The girls were on their hands and knees scrubbing floors with old tooth brushes and gallon metal "bean buckets" that canned vegetables and fruit came in. A matron had pulled the children out of their beds for giggling and laughing when they were supposed to be sleeping. It was hard for them to sleep when it was only 8:00 pm and it wasn't dark yet. It would be midnight before we would see our beds again. The smell of ammonia was making me dizzy.

A voice in my head reminded me, "You are an adult now. That was then; this is now."

I took a few deep breaths, turned on the radio, focused on the wind-shield wipers swishing back and forth and brought my thoughts back to the present moment. "Valerie, are you hungry? We haven't had breakfast yet."

Valerie replied "We had a granola bar on the train and I met a man who gave me a small bottle of wine last night. You wouldn't believe it, Sis; there were young mothers with kids that were crying, and I entertained them all the way here."

On the GPS, I located a McDonalds a few blocks from the train station. Valerie ordered a pancakes and scrambled eggs for her and Lilly to share. Paige and I each ordered an Egg Muffin with orange juice. When Valerie didn't reach for her purse to pay for the meal, I picked up the tab.

As we sat down and sipped our hot coffee and tea, Valerie rambled on and on about the train ride, talking faster than my brain could process what she was saying. "Hey Sis, I remembered that you were Dutch. Look what I bought for Paige."

As if pulling magic tricks out of a hat, she unearthed a Pennsylvania Dutch coloring book from her black handbag. Paige and Lilly got along splendidly and colored while Valerie talked and talked some more.

After breakfast, we took the girls to the Carnegie Science Center to walk around before the drive home. Valerie chattered about California. The girls were thirsty, so I bought two bottles of water. While sitting and watch-ing the girls climb a simulated rock wall, Valerie asked me "What made you want to pay for my trip here, Jeanette?"

"A few months ago, I started reading about the life of St. Francis. When we were talking on the phone, and you told me that you and Lilly were homeless and needed a place to stay, I thought about what St. Francis would have done. His teachings are that if someone needs a shirt, give him your shirt. Give whatever you have to someone in need." I replied.

"I couldn't believe it when I was standing on the streets of LA waiting for a bus, and you told me I could come to Pennsylvania and stay with you. I didn't have any other options. Does your husband treat you nice and how does he feel about us coming to stay with you? He sounds nice on the phone when I call." Cliff and I had just celebrated our tenth anniversary. When I told him about Valerie's plight he suggested that she come and stay with us.

"Cliff is supportive of you and Lilly coming and enjoys helping people out as much as I do. We hosted Asian exchange students for a couple of years, and even though it was challenging, he was supportive. The first time I told him about you was when we were hiking in a field nearby our house and had to go under a barbed wire fence. As he held the fence up for me, I told Cliff about the time you and I tried to run away from Mooseheart.

Valerie interrupted, "Sis, remember when we tried to run way, we were trying to get to Aurora?"

"How can I forget that? When Cliff and I first met, we were going through his family's old pictures; I came across a 1959 black and white photograph of two women holding little children at Baby Village in Mooseheart. When I questioned Cliff about the photographs, he recognized the ladies as his great aunts, Wilda and Ruth, but didn't know anything about the pictures. Just think Valerie, if the picture had been taken two years later, his aunts could have been holding us at Baby Village. Cliff wasn't sure why his aunts were at Mooseheart. We thought the puzzle was solved when we found letters sent back and forth between his Aunt Wilda and Aunt Ruth from Johnsonburg, Pennsylvania to Aurora, Illinois. I thought that when Aunt Ruth lived in Aurora and Aunt Wilda visited her, they took a trip to Mooseheart to see us orphans like people go to visit the zoo. Remember how visitors would tour the thousand-acre campus and throw coins on our beds?"

"Yeah, and the matrons gathered up all the money and kept it for themselves."

"The mystery was later solved when I was sorting through more photographs and came across a sepia toned photograph of a little girl in a hospital gown standing by an open window in front of a metal hospital bed. Her haircut and the gown she was wearing looked familiar. When I turned it over, the name June Clerkins was scrawled on the back.

I called Cliff at work to ask him if he knew June Clerkins. He said he didn't know but would find out. After calling some relatives, he learned that June was his cousin and her real name was Jeanette Frances Clerkins. Aunt Ruth took her two children to Mooseheart after her husband died of typhoid fever in 1928. The family was only at Mooseheart a year before Aunt Ruth remarried and they moved to Aurora. After leaving Mooseheart, "June" died of leukemia in her early thirties."

There was a moment of silence between us until I asked, "Have you been back to visit Mooseheart since we left, Valerie?"

"No, I just try to forget about the place. You?"

"Well, the family photos intrigued Cliff enough that he wanted to see where I lived as a child. I had pretty much put Mooseheart out of my mind until I started reading on the Moose website that they were asking for sixteen million dollars a year to support Mooseheart. There are only two hundred children there now, and you and I both know the kids aren't wearing designer clothes or driving BMW's.

Each time I drive by a Moose Club and see the words "Family Center" I want to scream. I wouldn't take my family there for all the tea in China. After finding June's picture and with Cliff's encouragement I decided to write a book and thought a trip to do some research might be helpful."

I went on to explain to Valerie, that in 2005 Cliff and I traveled out to Mooseheart for my thirtieth-class reunion and Mooseheart's annual homecoming. After the ten-hour drive, we stayed overnight at a Bed and Breakfast nearby. I slept restlessly, anticipating what tomorrow would be like. The next morning when we arrived at the thousand-acre complex, alumni were milling around the field house where registration was taking place.

After receiving my packet of information, including a program, name badge and map, I noticed in the program that there was an event going on at Baby Village. It was sponsored by Pennsylvania Moose Lodges and was scheduled to begin in just a few minutes. I excitedly told Cliff that was the first place I wanted to show him. We got in the car and drove over to Baby Village.

When we arrived at the little cul de sac with a heart shaped wading pool surrounded by four gray concrete, one story halls with red tiled roofs named after the rivers of Pennsylvania, ten pre-school children were sitting cross-legged on the ground in front of a nursery school waiting for the event to begin.

Orange plastic snow fencing blocked concrete sidewalks where steam was seeping out of the ground. As we waited for the program to start, I took the opportunity to introduce myself to a woman standing next to me.

"Hi, my name is Jeanette. Are you here for the alumni homecoming weekend?"

"No, I'm a family teacher."

"Oh, we used to call you matrons. How many children are in Baby Village now?"

"About ten kids."

"Do the children live with their siblings?"

"Oh no."

"So, they still separate the children. Are mothers still allowed to stay at Mooseheart?"

"They stopped that a long time ago."

Now, not only was steam rising out of the ground, I felt it welling up in my heart. As an adult, I learned that trust and attachment are the first phases of a child's development. When I was at Mooseheart, each year we moved to a different hall with different matrons caring for us, making it nearly impossible for us to form attachments.

John Bowlby, a medical doctor who himself was left with a nanny at an early age, extensively studied childhood attachment, separation and loss wrote, "If a child is taken from his mother's care at this age, when he is so possessively and passionately attached to her, it is indeed as if his world had been shattered."

I imagined that perhaps now, thirty years later, the place had evolved and the Moose members would have seen the wisdom in housing families together in the large halls. Instead, I felt as if time had traveled backwards.

A microphone crackled as a Moose member, dressed in a white dress shirt and tie began to speak. He welcomed the crowd and went on to brag about all the money that was donated to fix the antiquated boiler system. After his lecture, he told the children sitting cross-legged on the ground to clap their hands to thank the Pennsylvania Moose Clubs for fixing the heating system.

Again, I could feel the steam rising inside of myself. I raised my hand to ask why the children had to thank someone for fixing something that wasn't their fault. I also asked what they were going to do to fix the emotions that the children were bottling up from being separated from their siblings and parents. I pointed to Schukyill Hall and said that I was dropped off there in 1961 when I was three years old and was still healing from the trauma.

Cliff was surprised by my outburst and became concerned they would tar and feather me for speaking out, so he stood closely by my side."

Valerie clapped her hands and said, "Good for you, Sis."

"After the ceremony, we were walking to the field house for lunch and met two teenage boys standing in front of one of the halls. We stopped and chatted with them a few minutes. When I asked what they liked to do, they said they liked to sneak out of the halls to go night crawling. I was surprised to hear that term again."

"Sis, remember when we went out night crawling to the boy's campus with Tammy Ruple after Girl Scout meetings in the basement of Massachusettes Hall?"

"Yeah, I had a crush on Tom Fraling and we snuck our first kiss."

I went on to tell her that the boys told Cliff and me that now they have cameras in the halls and that the cameras shouldn't be for them, but for the 'Family Teachers.' I inquired if there was any abuse going on and they both shook their heads yes. A few months later someone sent me an article online from the Aurora Beacon News that a 'family teacher' was arrested for sexually abusing ten boys. Mooseheart isn't only a haven for children; it's a haven for child predators.

Even though I didn't have an appetite, we made it to the fieldhouse for a lunch of chicken and corn on the cob from the air-void containers. The smell of the food made me want to throw up. I told Cliff that I needed to go home. We drove straight back to Pennsylvania without stopping.

"I guess it's good I've never been back," Valerie replied.

Valerie had to use the restroom at the Carnegie Science Center, so I kept an eye on the girls. When she didn't return, I started to wonder what happened to her. I gathered up the girls and headed down the ramp to the lower floors. As I glanced down, she was meandering back up to the second floor. She looked so distant and far away. I asked myself what was I getting into and thought about how God watches over us from above. I prayed that He would watch over both Valerie and me.

On the drive home, we chatted about our childhood. She finished my sentences and I finished hers. For the first time in my life, I had someone to reminisce with about childhood memories. Although I have six other siblings, none of us had the same home. I was the caboose of seven and Valerie was next to the caboose of seventeen siblings. Valerie and I spent every day together for ten years of our childhood life. I felt as if I knew her better than I did my siblings.

As we drove through the mountains, the trees were tinged with colorful leaves just waiting to display their autumn splendor. Valerie said, "The cool air is refreshing and the trees are beautiful. I've always wanted to see Pennsylvania in the fall."

"I can't wait to see snow," Lilly shouted from the back seat.

Although clouds, heavy with rain, darkened the horizon, Valerie and I sang the same song in unison. "You are my sunshine, my only sunshine; you make me happy when skies are gray."

When we arrived at my little farm on four acres of land, nestled in the Allegheny National Forest, Valerie and Lilly were pleased with the comfortable setting of our home. Valerie talked about living on a farm in Indiana after she got kicked out of the orphanage. She questioned out loud, "Who would have thought that Jeanette Van Zanten would have ended up with a beautiful home like this?"

I drove Valerie and Lilly to the East Branch Dam for a hike to see the colored leaves that swirled down from the trees and to enjoy the smell of autumn while we walked through fallen leaves that rustled around our feet.

On Monday, we enrolled Lilly in the Ridgway Elementary School. I took Valerie to second hand shops so she could stock up on winter clothes for her and her daughter.

I found solace and comfort in quiet but discovered that Valerie preferred talking. She talked about everything; about movie stars in California, about dentistry, about the medical field, about her father and mother about whom I didn't know anything about, and about her brothers and sisters who didn't talk to her anymore. I didn't remember her talking so much at the orphanage, or did she?

It didn't take much for her to talk me into going with her to steal bars of soap at the dispensary and cigarettes from Mrs. Gilson, the 5th-grade girl's matron. She did talk me into tipping the canoes at the lake. When she talked me into crossing the railroad tracks with her to run away, she didn't have to twist my arm.

When caught, we had to stay in our beds for three days without anything to eat except peanut butter and jelly sandwiches, without the jelly. For more punishment, we were sent to the detention hall called the "farm," where we cleaned day and night and only had peanut butter sandwiches and hard-boiled eggs to eat.

Suddenly I felt like I was drowning. The same feeling of drowning in the wading pool at Baby Village when Valerie held my head under the water; I couldn't breathe. The same feeling of drowning I felt at camp when the counselors made us swim across the pool in jeans and a sweatshirt for relay races. I couldn't move my arms to swim any longer. The heavy wet clothes pulled me under the water. Finally, one of the counselors jumped in and pulled me out of the pool. Who was going to pull me out now?

Valerie cleaned my house with the old toothbrushes until it 'shined like the top of the Chrysler building' while I worked the 3-11 shift at an assisted living facility.

When on duty, I was instructed to call the supervisor for assistance. For the life of me, I couldn't dial the rotary phone when I needed help with a patient. At the same time, I was getting severe headaches.

When I asked myself where the fear and headaches were coming from, I had flashbacks of Valerie's head being split open with the hand piece of the black rotary phone by a matron. Blood gushed between her fingers as she held her head tight and screamed "Help me! Help me!" I cowered in the corner with my hands over my eyes and could feel my head splitting open, thinking that if I experienced the hurt, it would take Valerie's pain away.

The next day after Lilly left for her first day of school, I asked Valerie if she recalled the phone incident and she repeated it word for word as I remembered it. I thought I made stories like this up. After leaving Mooseheart, when I was thirteen years old, I shut out the experience, until one day when I was watching an Oprah Winfrey show, and she used the term incest. I had never heard the word before, but knew in an instant what it meant and that it had happened to me.

At the same time, John Bradshaw's book, *Homecoming* was released. Thinking I could heal myself, I began watching him speak about family dysfunction and abuse on PBS. I started seeing a family physician for depression and he suggested I see a psychologist.

I refused because I didn't want to be crazy like my mother. But the black hole of depression was swallowing me up, so I sought out counseling. After a few visits, the psychologist diagnosed me with Post Traumatic Stress and Multiple Personality Disorder that later was changed to a Dissociative Identity Disorder. Dr. Francis, the psychologist, explained that dissociating was a creative, unique way for me to survive my childhood, but it had it's challenges.

In the process of "splitting" to escape the trauma of being abandoned, neglected and abused, my identity fragmented. I was relieved to have an explanation as to why I could forget what happened to me as a child.

It also explained why I found myself in places without realizing how I got there, why my handwriting was inconsistent and why I experienced periods of rage when I felt as if I could kill myself or someone else, such as the time when I heard "Brat" come out of the mouth of my daughter's teenage friend. A rage swelled up from my gut. My blood began to boil and all the rage I held in for nearly thirty years exploded. I grabbed the snotty fifteen-year-old by the locks of her curly brown hair and took her out on the back porch and began to choke her. "Don't you ever call me that again," I screamed.

Out of the corner of my eye, I saw the other teens scatter like scared little kittens to the bedrooms in the back of the mobile home. After the rage had subsided, I felt like a piece of shit. I realized that I ruined my teenage daughter's sleep over. Moments earlier the five teenage girls and I were in the kitchen making homemade pizza. As we were stretching the dough onto the baking sheets, the conversation turned to nicknames.

Heather, the girl I nearly choked to death, asked: "Jeanette, did you have a nickname when you were little?"

Before I could change the subject, my daughter Brandi innocently said: "Yeah, her nickname was Brat." My parenting skills were quite weak, and I told Brandi to shut up.

If I had that moment to do over again, I would have said, "Brandi open the jar of pizza sauce." And when Heather called me Brat, I would have said, "Heather, the bag of mozzarella cheese is in the fridge."

But that's not how the story ended. I returned to the kitchen and finished the pizza myself without the girl's help. After everyone had finished eating, I told the girls to clean up the kitchen. I slipped on my shoes and took the keys to the car, not telling anyone where I was going or when I would be back.

In the pouring down rain, I jetted from the mobile home to where the car was parked a hundred yards away. I inserted the key into the ignition, started the engine, turned on the windshield wipers and backed the maroon hatchback down the long country driveway that turned onto Route 948.

I planned on driving a few miles up the road to cool off and have some time to myself. The windshield wipers were swishing back and forth, and the lights of a tractor trailer were coming toward me.

I was surprised by the voice in my head. "Turn into the front of the semi! Turn now, and it will all be over."

The car veered to the left and then I thought of my four children.

"Beeepppp!" The sound of the tractor trailer horn startled me and I swerved the car back across the double yellow lines and pulled over to the side of the road. I leaned my head on the steering wheel and sobbed for a half an hour.

I realized this was an over-reaction to a teenage girl calling me a name, but didn't understand why or what to do about it. I knew it was time to make an appointment with a psychologist.

Living in a rural area, every week I drove fifty-miles one way to the therapist. At the time, not only was I trying to parent four children without any parenting skills, but I was in an unhappy marriage and to top it off, I was a Jehovah's Witness.

Dr. Francis was compassionate and kind as he skillfully walked me through my childhood memories acknowledging the buried anger, hurt, and shame. He tried to help me integrate the memories and fragmented identities. The thought of integration was foreign as I had never experienced wholeness.

Dr. Francis used illustrations such as baking a cake, explaining that all the parts mattered, even the minuscule ones such as the baking powder and salt. When that didn't click, he used the illustration of individual baseball team players that all made up one team. Parts of me were afraid of getting lost in the integration process.

When the False Memory Syndrome became a fad in 1990's, a part of me thought Dr. Francis was eliciting memories-even though memories surfaced on their own, often as nightmares and flashbacks-and I was going along with him to get all the attention I lacked as a child. He tried to convince me otherwise because the stories were consistent with physical symptoms and I wasn't out to defame anyone.

I tried to go on with my life as if I had made everything up, but Valerie now confirmed that the memories were real. According to Greek Mythology, Pandora's Box is a box that contained all the evils of the world.

When Pandora opened the box, all the evils flew out, leaving only Hope inside once it was closed. Pandora's box was now wide open…

Chapter One

———•————————————•———

When three loud whistles blew, signaling that passengers could board the train, I had nothing to cling to but a filthy hanky that smelled of my daddy's sweat, and a paper ticket the lady gave me through bars that looked like a cage. As I stood on my tippy toes, she handed me a ticket and warned, "Don't lose this or you won't be able to get on the train."

Instead of holding a ticket, what I wanted was my gray, stuffed toy donkey named Pedro, my tabby cat Tissy and the crème colored musical rocking chair my daddy gave me for my third birthday. All these things were now just a memory.

The conductor, in a blue coat with gold buttons and a hat with a shiny black bill to match, bellowed, "All aboard to Chicago." I was wearing a pastel-colored dress and a blue and black plaid coat with fleece lining. A matching hat covered my ears and tied beneath my chin. When the line of people moved, I shuffled my black patent leather shoes along the worn, wood floor of the Pennsylvania train station.

I tried to cling to my mommy's carrot colored overcoat that felt like scratchy hay. From behind, I recognized my brother's familiar baritone voice mimic the porter, "All aboard the orphan train."

Tears welled up in my eyes when I couldn't see my mommy. My dark brown eyes looked up at the gray sky one last time before entering the passenger car and saw a blackbird circling the train I would be riding in for the next two days. I wanted to ride in a red caboose, but there wasn't one because this was a passenger train, not a freight train. The next loud whistle let out a scream, and my head felt like it was going to explode.

My sixteen-year-old sister, Ginny grabbed my arm and dragged me to the seat next to her on the train; my five brothers clamored for window seats. All seven of us children were wearing our new Easter clothes donated to us by the Sharon Moose Lodge. The boys sported tweed suit coats and dark colored slacks. Our few belongings, packed up in shiny black trunks with gold clasp buckles, were loaded on the train.

Click clack, click clack, click clack, the wheels on the train rumbled. The train passed trees without leaves and in time mountains were replaced by flat land with brown grass and clumps of snow. When I quit crying, a black man dressed in a uniform with double brass buttons and hat gave me a Peppermint Patty. I took a bite and the sweet mint taste made my stomach burn. As the train began to sway back and forth on the track, I became more nauseous and threw up all over my new clothes. Still, to this day, I detest Peppermint Patty candy.

When the dark replaced the light outside, the lightbulbs in the train flickered on and off. Ginny and I went to a car with bunk beds and clean sheets to sleep. She crammed me next to the wall, so I didn't fall off the bed.

Before I fell asleep she recited the words, "Now I lay me to sleep, I pray the Lord, my soul to keep. If I die before I wake, I pray the Lord, my soul, to take. God bless Daddy. God Bless Mommy. God bless our family. Amen."

The first time I heard about God, it wasn't from a pulpit. It was from my father's mouth after he came home from working the night shift at the Westinghouse factory.

With the smell of Blatz beer on his breath, he threw his aluminum lunch bucket on the counter and said: "God damn it, Dorothy, clean up this mess. And why the hell aren't these kids in bed sleeping?" The mess he wanted to be cleaned up was the dirty laundry, dirty dishes, and dirty floors of the two-story farmhouse, located on Clarksville Road in Sharpsville, Pennsylvania.

In 1920 my father, Paul Van Zanten, immigrated from Albasserdam, Holland when he was only nine years old. Holland, a country not much larger than the state of Rhode Island, was overcrowded and people were so poor they had to eat tulip bulbs to stay alive.

To escape the famine and the bombings from World War I, my Opa, Cornelius Van Zanten, my Oma, Elizabeth Roosenberg Van Zanten, and their four children boarded the ocean liner Kroonland from a seaport in Antwerp, Belgium.

My dad, Paul, his brother Jacob, and his twin sisters, Lena and Jeanette along with my Aunt Gerty sailed to America where there was more than enough air to breathe and land to farm. The Van Zanten family settled in Newton, Ohio where they lived in a two-story clapboard house and grew celery for a living.

True to his Dutch heritage, my father was self-reliant and independent. He met my mom, Dorothy Horstman at the Westinghouse plant. She was ten years younger than my dad and came from a large family of six. Together they saved enough money to buy fifty acres of land a few miles north of Sharpsville, Pennsylvania nestled in the Shenango Valley, just south of the Pymatuning Dam.

They purchased a two-story house, built by my dad's older brother Jake, located in a hollow next to my Oma's house. Gardening was in my father's blood, and he was particularly adept at growing strawberries for an additional source of income. Although he wasn't Catholic, my father was happy to have a large family, especially five sons, to help take care of the family farm, or so he thought. Within thirteen years, my parents had seven children.

I was the caboose, born at the Sharon, General Hospital in Sharon Pennsylvania. I weighed in at nearly nine pounds and with dark brown eyes and a head full of brunette hair. I was named Jeanette (God is Gracious) Elizabeth (Oath of God) Van Zanten after my aunt and Dutch grandmother.

My brother Warren, who everyone called 'Buddy' was two years older than me couldn't pronounce my name, so he nicknamed me Jo-Jo. When my sister Ginny heard that I was a girl, she was delighted to have a little sister instead of another little brother. I wasn't a planned child.

My mom was Catholic and didn't practice birth control or abortion. My oldest three siblings were baptized in the Catholic church, but after my father had an argument with the priest for some unknown reason, the last four children were baptized in the Presbyterian Church.

My parents brought me home from the hospital in a second-hand nightgown and a tattered blue blanket. I shared a room with my thirteen-year old sister, Ginny, who was about as moody as most teenagers are.

My crib had wooden slats, splattered with milk and engraved with teeth marks from each child that used it before me. A tabby cat named Tissy, lapped the milk from the dripping bottle that fell out of my mouth as I drifted off to sleep. Never did I fall asleep to the sound of a mother singing *Rock A Bye Baby,* but only to a cat purring by my head. My five brothers all slept in the same bed, in a bedroom next to ours. It was no picnic for them, especially when the younger one wet the bed. However, they were glad I wasn't a boy.

Even though it wasn't my sister's job to raise me, in the middle of the night when I woke up crying, she changed my wet cloth diaper, sometimes poking me with the safety pin. She wasn't the most careful person in the world and tossed me back into the crib and stuffed a bottle in my mouth to shut me up.

She had to get up for school in the morning and did her best to take care of me while my mother was out picking strawberries or having nervous breakdowns. Perhaps now, she would be treated for post-partum depression. Thankfully, my father noticed we weren't being cared for and hired Mary Bowman, a seventeen-year-old girl to take care of us.

Mary was a pretty girl with golden blonde curls that came down to her shoulders. Her sparkly, bright eyes made me coo when she smiled and talked to me. In the evening, she rocked me to sleep singing Hush Little Baby. As I was falling asleep, the cat tried to sneak up on Mary's lap. Quietly, she put the end of the bottle under her chin and pushed the cat onto the floor. At night, she would shut the door to my room so the cat couldn't get into my crib.

Once, Mary tended to a sore on my right thigh. When she asked the boys what happened, they told her the cat spilled toilet cleaner on my leg. The truth was, I had crawled into the bathroom and opened a can of drain cleaner and spilled it on my leg. The caustic substance burnt a hole in my leg, down to the bone.

My parents refused to take me to the hospital for the burn. Everyday Mary changed the white bandage and dabbed orange mercurochrome on the sore until it healed. When I tried to pull off the scab, she rubbed it with my Oma's ointment made from Vaseline and camphor.

Oma, Opa and Aunt Gerty lived in a house about one hundred yards north of our farm house. Oma was a stern woman who wasn't very happy with our mother's lack of care for us.

She compensated by bringing us large pots of hutspot, a Dutch dish of mashed potatoes, carrots, and turnips, home baked bread, jars of pickled herring and bags of Zout, a black, salty licorice from Holland. At Christmas, she baked Speculass cookies, and on New Year's Day she made a washtub full of fried doughnut balls with apples and raisins, called Olie Bollen.

After my dad had hired Mary, we had more to eat than boiled macaroni. She prepared toast and eggs for breakfast and soup and sandwiches for lunch. Mary knew how to take charge of my brothers. She washed the dirty sheets from their bed and hung them out on the line to dry.

On Saturday nights, she filled the cast iron claw bathtub with warm water. She would yell, "You boys get in here one at a time and get scrubbed up for church tomorrow."

When the older boys laughed about putting mud on my three-year-old brother Warren's baby bottle and told him it was chicken poop, Mary scolded them and washed off his bottle, although he never used it again.

The boys taunted her "Mary, Mary, quite contrary, why don't you get out of our home?" Even though they didn't like her as much as Ginny and I did, we celebrated her and my brother Jack's birthdays together in late September.

When Mary was at the house, my daddy didn't say "God damn it" so much. The swearing resumed after the mailman knocked on the door of the yellow brick farm house.

Knocks and locks on doors were foreign in the 1950's. People came and went, but no one ever knocked on the door. My ten-year-old brother Paul was home from school, recovering from a bout of rheumatic fever and answered the door. When he opened the front door of the house, the postman dressed in a blue uniform asked: "Is your dad home, son?"

"No, my mom is sleeping, and my dad is working."

"I need Paul Van Zanten's signature on this letter."

"My name is Paul Van Zanten."

"Well, I guess you will have to do." The postmaster handed him a slip of yellow paper and a pen attached to a clipboard. "Sign your John Henry by the X.

"But my name is Paul Henry."

"It's just a saying son. Write Paul Henry on the line."

Paul scrawled his name on the paper and handed it back to the mail carrier. In return, he handed my oldest brother a letter that changed our family's fate. Paul put the letter on the kitchen table and finished the erector set he was building in the living room.

When daddy returned home from work, Paul ran to give him the letter that he had signed for that day. After setting down his stainless-steel thermos of black coffee on the table, Daddy slid his hands into the pocket of his Dickies navy blue, canvas work pants for his pocket knife. He slit the top of the envelope open and read the letter. With his eyebrows furrowed and deep creases across his forehead, he raised his left hand to the shadowy stubble on his face and asked, "What the hell?"

"What's the matter, daddy? Did I do something wrong?" Paul asked with his voice shaking.

"No son, you didn't do anything wrong. It's that damn government. I'm going to get the lawyer on the phone."

My dad unearthed the phone directory from beneath a stack of papers and looked up the attorney's number. He dialed the number, one brrrr, for each number on the dial. When a woman answered the phone, he ordered: "Put Casik on the phone."

"Hello Mr. Van Zanten, what can I do for you?"

"You can tell me what this God damn letter is about."

"Who's it from and what does it say?"

I started to cry and crawled over to my daddy's legs for him to hold me.

"God Damn it, Dorothy, get his kid off my leg and get these kids out of the kitchen. I need to talk on the phone."

Ginny ran over and grabbed me by the arm and dragged me out of the kitchen into the living room.

"The letter is from the U.S. Government, and it read:

Dear Mr. Van Zanten,

We are writing to inform you that plans are being finalized for installation of the Shenango Lake to prevent the future flooding of the Shenango Valley. This flood control project will not only save many lives, but it will offer recreation opportunities to thousands of Pennsylvania and Ohio Residents. As you can see from the attached map, your property on Clarksville Road lies in the designated area for the projected lake.

Therefore, the United States Government will purchase your property under eminent domain. You will be given a fair market property value to move your home to a different property outside of the projected flood plane."

Sincerely,

U.S. Government

The whole house settled down. I had never heard that much quiet in my whole life.

My father broke the silence: "God dam it are you there?"

The lawyer replied, "I'm sorry Mr. Van Zanten, but the letter is stating that the government will be seizing your property for the flood control project."

"What the hell is wrong with these damn Americans. Don't they know about windmills to control flooding? We should have never come to this damn country."

"Mr. Van Zanten, I will work hard to make sure you get fair market value for your house."

"What the hell do you mean fair market value? How can anyone reimburse the hours of labor I have into tilling the land for the strawberries I grow and sell."

My brother Paul became nervous that Daddy would start beating on my mom again, so he ran up to Oma's to tell her about the letter he should have never signed for. Oma was sitting in the kitchen with her wire-framed eyeglasses on her lap; tears were streaming down her bony cheeks. The same letter that Daddy received in the mail was on Oma's handcrafted oak kitchen table. Paul had never seen Oma cry before, but he didn't feel like it was his fault, because he didn't sign for her letter.

Eighty-two other homeowners in the Shenango Valley received the same notice. The proposed Shenango Dam was one of sixteen flood control projects in the Pittsburgh District of Western Pennsylvania authorized by the Flood Control Acts of 1938 that would devastate people's lives, including their school, their church, and a cemetery. Over two hundred people gathered at the local grange hall to stop the government from building the dam. They argued that the land was fertile farmland utilized to grow crops.

The government argued that the dam would save millions of dollars in flood damage to the city of Sharon. People became bitter because the Pymatuning Dam that had been built in 1934 was supposed to prevent flooding.

During the summer, the reservoir was filled with water for boating and fishing. In the winter the water was drained to allow for spring water to fill the dam and prevent flooding. In 1958, a summer flood finalized plans for the Shenango Valley Dam. The dam was full of water for recreation purposes, and water flooded the city of Sharon, costing millions of dollars. Engineers determined that another dam should be built to prevent flooding.

Farmers and landowners were told that they would receive millions of dollars for their land that would be used as a tourist resort. Only one in eight farmers made out financially. Other farmers, such as the Jewell family who attended the same Presbyterian church as our family, received a paltry $21,000 for two hundred acres of farmland, a house, and outbuildings. Their land was never flooded or made into a resort, and they never received millions of dollars for their property. According to John Jewell, who was twenty-eight at the time, "The government stole our land, and people became bitter."

That summer, when school was out, Daddy loaded a flat bottom aluminum fishing boat on top of the green 1958 station wagon and headed to Canada for a fishing trip with my two oldest brothers, Paul, and Bill.

Before they left, he said, "Dorothy, start cleaning out this house and packing our things. I'm going to Canada to see if I can find a place for us to live. I've had enough of living in this God Damn country."

When the crew returned from Canada with enough walleye and musky to fill our freezer, daddy was more hopeless and depressed. He told our mom, "There's nothing up in Canada that we can afford.

Daddy quit coming home after work at night and began spending more and more time at the Moose Club with his drinking buddy Fred who, ironically later became one of my mom's boyfriends. Instead, he came home in the early morning hours, just before sunrise. Clump, clump, clump, I could hear his footsteps coming up the steps. And then the yelling began; "God Damn it Dorothy, where the hell is my supper? There isn't a bite of food in this house."

One Friday, on a Memorial Day weekend, the phone rang at about the same time my father usually came stumbling in from the bars. After five rings, my mom lifted the receiver and said, "Hello."

"Mrs. Van Zanten, this is the Sharon General Hospital. Your husband has been in an accident and we would like you to come to the hospital to sign papers as soon as possible."

"But I don't drive, and I can't come to the hospital."

"Mrs. Van Zanten, is there a relative that you can call? Your husband is in very serious condition."

After my mom had hung up the phone, she told Paul, who had now turned eleven, to ride our pony Bonnie up to Uncle Henry's, our dad's brother, and tell him that Daddy was in an accident. My mom couldn't call because Uncle Henry's wife Aunt Evelyn wouldn't answer the phone.

Within an hour, Uncle Henry pulled in our driveway driving his 1940 navy blue pickup truck with Aunt Evelyn by his side and Paul riding in the back. Paul hopped out of the truck and said: "I'm going to the hospital with you Mom."

Aunt Evelyn slid her legs out the passenger side of the truck and said, "Oh no you aren't young man. You are staying right here with me until your Uncle Henry, and Mom get back from the hospital." Paul knew it's a hopeless case to argue with Aunt Evelyn.

My father's lung was punctured in the accident. He returned home to convalesce. A few months later, on November 6, 1960, my father died in the Warren General Hospital, in Warren Ohio. If my mom couldn't take care of us before, she surely couldn't take care of us now.

There wasn't money to pay Mary to manage us. My mom would shoo my six and seven-year-old brothers, Jack and Bob out of the house on more than one occasion, telling them "Go over to Uncle Henry's house and help him with the sheep."

The boys hiked the ten-mile road by themselves. When they arrived at Uncle Henry's, he asked, "What are you boys doing over here by yourselves? If Aunt Evelyn sees you, she will call the police. You go on home and instead of walking the road back, go through the field. It will be shorter."

A lady named Sue Subasic came and took my brother Jack off of my mom's hands. Jack's nickname was "Nuisance" as he had a knack for getting himself or someone else into trouble. Instead of going to the funeral he stayed with the Subasic family.

My older brothers, Paul and Bill, took over the farm animals and started killing the cats, including Tissy, by pouring gas on their tails and lighting them on fire. Uncle Henry stepped in and took the pony, Bonnie, and our collie before they were harmed. When my brother Paul heard talk of all of us going to Mooseheart, he threatened to run away.

When the 1948 yellow bus arrived each morning to pick the older kids up for school, I stared out the window and cried. I didn't like being home alone with my mommy who slept on the couch all day and didn't get up to feed me. Friends and neighbors brought us groceries. The Sharon Moose Lodge made sure we had a good Christmas by bringing gifts and food.

Before my father passed away, he signed the necessary papers for our house to be sold and moved. A realtor offered him $25,500 for our two-story farm house and fifty acres of land. My father made out a will stating that the money would be shared between my mom and their seven children.

The proceeds were put in a trust that we would receive when we turned eighteen. With the money tied up in a trust, my mother couldn't buy any property to start anew. The Shenango Valley Lake was due to be completed in 1965 and allegedly prevented millions of dollars of flood damage to the city of Sharon.

My father also took advantage of an insurance policy from the Moose Club. Mooseheart was one of the perks of joining the Moose Club. If a member passed away, he was insured that his young children and spouse could go to Mooseheart to live. In 1913, before foster homes and government assistance, James J. Davis, opened the institution to provide a home for children and mothers of deceased Moose Members.

In January, 'Uncle Leo' drove my mom out to Mooseheart to sign the necessary admission papers and to see where we would be living. When they returned to Pennsylvania, both of them raved about the beautiful Mooseheart Campus.

According to Judith Viorst, author of *Necessary Losses*, when a loss or death happens at such an early age, the emotional scars are similar to those of being doused with gasoline and lit on fire.

My father's death at an early age, changed how I would view the world. I lacked trust and had a deep sense of shame. Just when I was developmentally making attachments to my family, life was shattered by the death of my father and the loss of our home.

Chapter Two

———•————————————•———

The sun was rising as the train arrived at the Dearborn station in Chicago. When I stepped off the train, a gust of wind nearly swept me off my feet. I clung to my sister's dress as we shuffled single file, from the train into the station. A thin, squirrelly man wearing an overcoat and newsboy hat with a camera hanging around his neck said, "You kids are going to be in the Chicago Tribune." He crowded us together in the corner of the train station and flashed the camera. After the photo session, he jingled a set of keys and asked, "Do you kids want to go for a ride?"

Paul, answered, "Hell no, but give me the keys and I'll drive that jalopy."

When the man saw that the boys weren't going to get in the car willingly, he barked, "Get in the car. Two little ones up front with the mom." I sat on my mom's lap, and Warren sat between her and the driver. Bob and Jack scrambled into the back of the station wagon, and Bill, Paul, and Ginny sat in the middle seat. The black trunks with our belongings were piled into another car. Once we arrived at Mooseheart, we were dropped off at a large building, called a hall.

The minute we got out of the station wagon, a cross looking lady wearing a plaid cotton dress that buttoned up the front, nylons, and black oxfords, started barking orders. "You boys carry this luggage." When we entered the hall, that felt hollow and empty; her voice echoed off the walls as she talked. "Boys sleep on the right wing and girls on the left." For two weeks, we lived in quarantine.

My mom, Ginny and I followed her down a hallway to our bedroom, which was a dormitory. Even though I was three years old, she looked at my mom and said, "The little one will sleep in the crib. You and your daughter will sleep in these two beds," as she pointed to plastic covered mattresses with a set of white sheets, a blanket, bedspread, and pillow. "The beds need to be made before lunch. We eat at 12:00 p.m. when the whistle blows. I'll take the little one in to get cleaned up."

From that minute on, my mother or sister no longer had a say in my care. The matron stripped me of my clothes and put me in a bathtub. She scrubbed my skin with Fels Naptha soap, and scrub brushed me like I was a dog with fleas. I was dressed in issued clothing stamped with a laundry number. My laundry number-V1710-a number stamped not only on my clothes but also on my psyche. A number I would never forget.

When the matron and I returned to the bedroom, and she saw the sloppily made beds, she called for my mom and Ginny, who were sitting on the sofa in the living room. "Where did you people come from?" she asked as she stripped the beds. She then instructed them how to make a bed correctly by tucking in the sheets and making square corners.

The matron instructed the boys to wash their hands before she taught them how set the table. After we were finished eating, she gave them a lesson on how to wash, dry and put away the dishes.

At night when it was time to go to bed she lifted me up and put me in the crib. I hadn't slept in a crib for over a year now, so when she left, I hiked my legs up over the rail and dropped onto to the floor where I looked for a place to sleep. After dark, the matron returned with a flashlight for a bed check and found me asleep on the floor. She put me back in the crib, and with long white strips of cloth, I was tied to the rails.

The next day, we were taken to the beauty shop, where a teenage girl chopped my thin, scraggly hair into a short bob. My mom said I looked like a little Dutch girl. After that, we went to the hospital. I had never been to a doctor. A lady in a white dress gave me shots, including a small pox vaccine that hurt and left a scar on my right arm. The dentist was the next stop. He instructed me, "Open wide." When I opened my mouth wide, he stuck a wooden stick in my mouth, and said, "This one is going to need a lot of work."

On Sunday, we all dressed in our newly issued clothes and the squirrelly man came to the hall to take a family picture. The glossy black and white picture would be sent back to the Sharon Moose Lodge to show the members how well we were doing at Mooseheart.

After two weeks of indoctrination, the matron lined us up in a row. The boy's dean and the girl's dean each rattled off our names and the name of an assigned hall. The boy's dean begins, "Paul and Bill will be living in California Hall on the high school boy's campus. Robert, to New Jersey Hall, Jack to Greater Chicago Hall and Warren to Georgia-Alabama Hall."

My mother interrupted at this point. "I was told that Bob and Jack would be in the same hall together."

"Well, Mrs. Van Zanten, I don't know who told you that, but I'm the one in charge here, and the two boys will not be in the same hall together. They are nothing but trouble together. If you don't like it, take it up with the superintendent."

My mother fell back in line and didn't say another word. Upon admission to Mooseheart, she signed over our social security checks and all of her parental rights. She didn't have any say in our health care, discipline or education. Mooseheart called all the shots.

My mom wasn't alone in this situation. Some mothers were pregnant when they went to Mooseheart and after they had given birth, the infant stayed at the hospital until it started walking and then was transferred to a hall where a matron took care of the child.

The girl's Dean continued, "Virginia you will be going to Massachusetts Hall. And I want to make it clear that girls are not allowed on the boys' campus. If this rule is broken, you will be punished. Jeanette will be going to Schuylkill Hall at Baby Village."

Tears welled up in Ginny's red eyes and she told the dean, "Jeanette needs to be with me so I can take care of her."

"Virginia, you will not be taking care of your little sister. You can thank your lucky stars that you are even at Mooseheart. I don't know how you got in here, but sixteen-year-old girls aren't admitted to Mooseheart. Get your box of clothing and come with me."

No one thought to ask where our mom was going to live. Each one of us assumed she would be living with us. We didn't know that she would be living in a three-story cement block building called Loyalty Hall that is neither on the boy's campus or the girl's campus. She would be put to work at the laundry and cooking in the halls. We could visit her one hour each day and three hours on Sunday.

The boy's dean instructed the boys to gather up their boxes of clothing. They piled into a station wagon and were dropped off at their respective halls. The station wagon returned empty. Ginny, my mom and I got into the car that dropped my mom and me off at Baby Village.

We followed the sidewalk to a gray stone building that looked like thunderclouds, with a red tile roof. I counted the concrete steps. "One, two three," up to the red-tiled porch. My mom opened the white wooden gate and knocked on the door. An older woman with graying hair opened the paned glass door with a brass doorknob and said, "Hello. You must be Mrs. Van Zanten."

My mommy pulled her hand out of my little hand and looked down at me. "This lady is Mrs. Cox and she will be taking care of you from now on." I tried to hang on tightly to her hand, but she pushed me forward to the strange lady.

"Hi Jeanette, I'm Mrs. Cox, but you can call me Mommy Cox. Would you like to play with the other little girls?" I never played with other little girls. I only played in the mud with my brother, my cat, and my dog. I crossed my arms and shook my head back and forth.

After pushing me forward towards the lady, my mommy turned around and walked away, leaving me all alone in this strange place. I cried and cried and cried. The other little girls came over to comfort me. I didn't know how I was going to have two mommies, so I decided that since I'm wasn't going to be living with my real mommy, Mommy Cox would be my mommy.

After I quit crying, Mommy Cox allowed me to go outside for playtime. In the center of Baby Village, there was a cement wading pool, a cement block nursery school with a red tile roof, surrounded by four matching halls named after Pennsylvania rivers. Schuylkill and Alleghany Hall were for the preschool girls, Juniata and Susquehanna for the preschool boys. In the afternoon after our nap and before supper, we went outside to ride tricycles and red metals cars with pedals and on the playground with swings, a sliding board, and merry-go-round.

Schuylkill Hall was a sharp contrast from the filth and disorder of where I lived before. The floors were clean. I didn't have to wade through piles of shoes, papers, and garbage to walk down the hallways. The shiny glass windows, without muddy handprints and smudges from animals coming in and out, were cleaned weekly with ammonia.

In fact, there weren't any dogs or cats in this house. There weren't any chickens running around the yard. The windows had pretty curtains with flowers and weren't wrinkled or torn. In the living room, a few toys were neatly placed in a corner. In the center of the room, there was a big box with a glass front and knobs on the side. Sometimes the box talked and sang a song called *Pop Goes the Weasel*.

The dining room was nice and clean with places set for each child. It wasn't cluttered with leftover food, dirty dishes and cats weren't sitting on the table lapping up milk. In the kitchen, everything had a place. The white porcelain sink was clean; the floors were shiny, the trash was emptied, nothing was out of place.

My right thigh was still sensitive from the burn that happened when I was two years old. But when Mommy Cox took me into the bathroom, there wasn't any lye to hurt me. And I didn't have to worry about falling into the little pink porcelain toilets that were sparkling clean, without any brown stuff floating in the water.

I had to stand on a step stool to climb into the high bathtub so Mommy Cox could scrub me up and wash my hair once a week. There weren't any clothes piled up on the floors in the bedroom. The dressers had drawers for our clothes.

Eight neatly made little beds with sheets, blankets, pillows, and bedspreads were evenly spaced apart in the bedroom; there weren't any bare mattresses to sleep on here. Every night, the other little girls and I folded down the chenille bedspread to the bottom of the bed. The stiff white top sheet and blanket were turned back to a triangle. Before we climbed into bed, we knelt on the cold marble floors and folded our hands.

Peggy, Kathy, Valerie, Tammy and myself repeated after Mommy Cox, "Now I lay me down to sleep; I pray the Lord, my soul to keep. If I die before I wake, I pray the Lord, my soul, to take. Amen." When we woke, we made our beds. The matron showed us how to smooth the wrinkles out of the sheets.

To this day, I have a fetish for making my bed every day with perfect square corners and no wrinkles in the sheets or blankets.

In the afternoons, we took long naps in our little beds with railings, but I felt fidgety and restless, so pulled strings out of the blankets and taught myself how to make a chain stitch with the string. My bed was next to an open window, and I could hear birds chirping from the large Dutch Elm trees that swayed in the wind.

Although Mommy Cox tried to be nice to me, it was hard because there were other children that she cared for. I didn't like playing with the other children and I didn't want to share toys.

When Mommy Cox made me share, I got mad and sometimes tried to bite the other children. Mommy Cox sent me to my bed until I could behave. I looked at the curtains with pictures of Jack and Jill, Humpty Dumpty, Little Bo-Peep and Jack Be Nimble on them and snuggled my blanket and sucked my thumb until I could fall asleep.

Being alone in my bed was where I felt safe. Once, when I was in bed for not sharing, I heard a loud noise outside. It was summertime, and the windows were open. I knelt up on my bed and pressed my face against the screen, to see a big white truck with large black wheels going very slowly down the street, spraying water as it passed by Schuylkill Hall. I kept my eyes on the truck until it disappeared out of site.

The hum of the engine and the sound of the spray were soothing. I looked forward to seeing the visitor and began calling the spray truck Parker.

I tried to tell Mommy Cox about my friend Parker, but she scolded, "That truck isn't your friend, Jeanette. It's spraying all the bad bugs that eat the leaves off the trees." Mommy Cox didn't know then that the Dutch Elm trees were being sprayed with DDT, a toxic pesticide that would eventually be banned.

As summer was ending, I noticed familiar bugs that lit up and flashed on and off. While in my bed, one of the bugs flew through a hole in the screen and landed on my pillow and began to talk to me. "Hi, my name is Maly. What's your name?"

In a soft whisper, so that Mommy Cox couldn't hear me, I replied, "Jeanette." And then asked, "Why didn't Parker get rid of you? He is supposed to kill all the bad bugs."

"I'm not a bad bug," replied Maly. "I'm a good bug, and one of my jobs is to help you be happy. You seem very sad whenever you are looking out the window."

"I'm not sad; I'm mad," I replied.

"Why?" asked Maly.

"I don't like it here. Mommy Cox sends me to my bed all the time because I'm a bad girl." I tried to stop the tears, but they slid down my cheeks.

"Let me sing you a song before you go to sleep." I don't know how Maly knows my favorite song, Hush Little Baby, but the voice sounds like the lady Mary that took care of me before my daddy died. When Maly ends the song with the last verse, "You're still the sweetest little girl in town," I ask the bug, "At night I get afraid and lonely. Will you keep your light on and stay here with me?"

"Sure," said Maly.

The next morning when I woke up, the bug was gone. At the breakfast table, I excitedly began to tell Mommy Cox about the good bug that Parker didn't kill.

Mommy Cox scolded me, "That's just your imagination, be quiet and eat your cereal."

Along with my cereal, I swallowed my words and learned it was best not to speak my truth. I decided not to talk to Mommy Cox about Maly or Parker anymore. Each night Maly came flying on the screen and talked to me. I secretly whispered to Maly that Mommy Cox didn't treat me nice sometimes.

After all the leaves turned colors and fell off the trees, Parker didn't come by anymore. Maly flew in the room one more time to say good bye for the summer and told me she would see me again in the spring when the flowers were growing and the leaves were on the trees.

I began to rely more on my imagination than on the reality of Mooseheart.

The image of the white fence and the brick porch at Schuylkill Hall was imprinted in my mind. The abandonment of my mother was imprinted in my heart.

Ironically, the word Schuylkill, meaning Hidden River, originated from the Netherlands Dutch. John Bowlby, a 20th century psychologist, studied child development, and verified the deep impact abandonment had on a children. Although my mother was physically present in my life, I emotionally detached from her and would keep her at a distance the rest of my life.

Chapter Three

———•———————————————•———

The first movie I watched on television was The Wizard of Oz. The show came on once a year, and I watched it every year at the same time, for the next ten years. After supper, before it was dark outside, we changed into our pajamas. As we sat cross-legged on the floor, Mommy Cox turned on the black and white television.

The wicked witch and the monkeys terrified me, but it didn't take much for me to fall in love with Dorothy when she sang *Somewhere Over the Rainbow* and *A Few of my Favorite Things*. When I heard her voice, I felt my troubles melt like lemon drops, and at bedtime, I dreamed about bluebirds and rainbows. My mom's name was Dorothy, and I wished she could sing and look as pretty as the girl on TV.

More than anything, I wished I had a pair of red shoes that could take me home to see my Uncle Henry, who lived in Pennsylvania instead of Kansas. And I had an Aunt Velma, my mom's sister, who sounded almost like Auntie Em. My Uncle Henry was just as nice as Dorothy's Uncle Henry. And even though Aunt Velma wasn't nearly as kind as Dorothy's Auntie Em, I still missed her and wished I could see them both again. I hoped that I would wake up one morning and find that living at Mooseheart was just a dream.

When I turned four, I was moved to Allegheny Hall, and Mommy Cox didn't take care of me anymore. The first day in the new hall, a lady called a matron told me "I'm not your mommy, so don't call me mommy. My name is Mrs. Quillen."

The only thing that was the same was the little girls who moved with me. I celebrated my fourth birthday in Allegheny Hall. When all the children sang "Happy Birthday, Dear Jeanette," I began sobbing and hid my face in my folded arms. I wanted to run away and hide in a corner somewhere, but couldn't free myself from the high chair that I was buckled into.

My love of books and reading began when I went to nursery school during the day. Mrs. Brown, a tall, thin woman, who wore her brunette hair piled on top of her head, read a story to us before naptime.

The book I liked best was The Little Engine that Could. When Mrs. Brown gave me a wood shoe with laces and sat me in the corner until I could learn how to tie, I thought of the words; I think I can, I think I can, I think I can until I did. I liked putting the wooden puzzles together and eating graham crackers and milk for a snack.

At the nursery school, there was a special room where we took turns getting our pictures taken for the Moose Lodges. For my picture, I wore an army green corduroy dress with a white blouse underneath. The day before, my hair was cut at the beauty shop. In the picture room, white painted, wooden shelves held brand new toys that we couldn't reach.

When I saw all the toys, I thought the train from *The Little Engine that Could* must have dropped off all the toys for us children. Mrs. Brown reached up and took a toy off the shelf and handed it to me. I thought she was going to let me play with it; instead, a camera flashed.

While I rubbed my eyes, she took the toy and returned it to the shelf and told me to go back to the classroom with the other children. The glossy picture was published in the Moose Magazine and sent to the Moose Lodge to show the members how happy we were with the new toys they bought for us.

Little boys went to nursery school and it was fun playing with them. One of the boys named Percy, was Mooseheart's curly head mascot. He was chosen because he looked like a picture of a little boy with curly hair kneeling beside his bed with his hands folded saying his prayers, with the stately Campanile clock in the background. The Moose thought Percy needed more curls so he went to the beauty shop to have curls put in his hair. He then visited Moose Clubs and had his picture taken with the Moose members. I don't think Percy liked having his hair curled.

On weekends, if I didn't cry, I was allowed to visit my mom for an hour a day and three hours on Sunday. My older sister picked me up at Baby Village and walked me to visit my mom at Loyalty Hall. My mom made friends with Mrs. Gilson, Mrs. Harvey, Mrs. Hunden and Mrs. Stuckey, who were other mothers that lived at Loyalty Hall. They each had their room but shared a kitchen and a pay telephone that hung on the wall in the hallway. Just like my mom, the women worked in the halls cooking and cleaning.

Other mothers lived in rooms scattered throughout the campus, where they were away from their children. In exchange for the mother's free room and board, the women worked laboriously in the industrial laundry or as nurses at the hospital. Some were trained as nurse's aides, secretaries, and phone operators. Just like the children, the mothers were under the superintendent's thumb.

In the early days of Mooseheart, mothers weren't allowed to have cars or male visitors and weren't allowed off campus after dark or overnight, except with special permission. When my grandma died, my mom was able to return to Pennsylvania for her mom's funeral. Much to my mom's dismay, the children weren't allowed to attend; no if's, ands or buts were accepted.

Many of these unwritten rules lingered into the 1960's when mothers were still permitted to live at Mooseheart with their children. Some of the women exerted their independence by dressing in black and sneaking off campus at night through the cornfields, where they found night jobs waitressing, saving enough money to get themselves and their children out of Mooseheart. My mom didn't have that constitution.

All my brothers and sister visited our mom at the same time in the little room just big enough for a bed and a couch and a white metal cabinet where she kept a bottle of Mogan David wine, Dutch hot chocolate, rye bread and pickled herring. On Sundays, my mom drank the sweet, grape Mogan David wine. She didn't mind that we finished off the bottle that she left open.

Not all kids had a mom to visit an hour a day. They thought I was lucky having a mom, but I thought it was hard going to visit her for just an hour a day and saying goodbye all over again. When I kissed her good-bye, her cheek felt cold and sad. When I returned to the hall smelling like wine and pickled herring, the matron brushed my teeth and gave me a bath, even though it wasn't scheduled. All the while she bitched about how sick and tired she was of taking care of other people's kids.

On Sunday afternoons while I visited my mom, she did laundry using a wringer washer in the dank, dark basement of Loyalty Hall. While she was hanging up aprons in another room, I watched the agitator go swish-swash, swish-swash back and forth. I climbed on a step stool and reached in the washer and fished out an apron with pink and yellow flowers and put it in the wringer. I didn't know to let go of the apron, and my hand got caught in the wringer. I let out a scream, and my mom came running to see what happened.

I didn't know how I got to the hospital but remembered returning to the hall with my left hand bandaged in white gauze, where the matron sponge bathed me and asked why my mom couldn't even take care of me for a few hours. She wondered what was wrong with her that she made me do her laundry.

When the bandage was removed, there was a scar on my hand and whenever I got confused about which way was left or right, I looked down at my hand with the scar and knew which way was left. I wasn't allowed to see my mom for a few weeks, but when I saw her again, I wondered like the matron did, what was wrong with her.

Other times when I visited my mom, she let me iron clothes with a hot iron. I watched her use a white plastic bottle with a red rose on top to sprinkle water on the clothes to get the wrinkles out. It was then that I decided I liked the name Rose better than Jeanette. Rose didn't get hurt so much and didn't feel pain. When I returned to the hall and the matron hollered at me, I no longer felt frightened.

When I turned five years old, I left the safe confines of Baby Village and moved into a much larger building called Muncie Hall. There was a dormitory on one end of the hall and a dining and kitchen area on the other end.

Every Saturday was the same for me and the other five and six-year-old girls that lived in the yellow brick one story hall, with a cold concrete basement and over twenty shiny windows that were cleaned with ammonia and crumpled newspapers once a month.

At 6:30 a.m. a whistle blew to wake us up. It wasn't a shrill whistle like a policeman uses to direct traffic. It was a deep, long tone, more like that of a tug boat or a train that was arriving at the depot. The whistle could be heard by the three hundred or so other orphans, in thirty different halls throughout the thousand-acre campus. The whistle was the timekeeper. It told us not only when to wake, but when to leave for school when to eat dinner, when it was time for supper and when to go to bed at night.

When the morning whistle blew, our feet hit the cold marble floors of the dormitory. We retrieved our slippers from under the dresser and made our single beds, lined up next to each other like soldiers in a row. The stern matron reminded us not to talk or whisper. I was convinced she had an extra set of ears.

Valerie ignored the matron and whispered to me, "Hey sis, help me with my bed." Out of the corner of my eye, I saw the matron turn her head toward us.

Valerie wasn't my real sister, but we felt like sisters because we lived together at the orphanage since we were both three years old. We both arrived in 1961. I came from Pennsylvania; she hailed from Indiana.

When we made our beds, Valerie couldn't get the wrinkles smoothed out of the sheets and blanket like I could. She didn't have the same tension in her hands that I did. The tension required to make a perfectly square corner to tuck the sheet underneath the mattress, so it didn't come loose when we tossed and turned at night. Valerie didn't have the tension needed to tie a shoelace taunt and tight, nor the tension needed to fold a napkin square, so the corners met perfectly, and it laid flat underneath the fork at the table. She didn't have the tension that robbed me of sleep at night.

"Valerie, get that bed made instead of running at the mouth." After being scolded again, Valerie was left on her own to smooth the wrinkles out of her bed. When the beds were perfectly made and inspected, we fell in a single line and walked to the bathroom, our slippers scuffing across the floor, to use the porcelain toilets. The flushing water, in timed unison, told the matron how long we took to use the toilet. "Move it!" she hollered if one of us was a little slow and needed to do more than pee.

After using the bathroom, we walked in line back to the dormitory to change our clothes. I folded the sleeves of my cotton pajamas, so the seams lined up. I tucked the neat package underneath the pillow on my bed. I left on my white undershirt and panties that I only changed at night and then retrieved the week's play clothes from the bottom dresser drawer. I slipped on a plaid, short sleeve blouse, and counted the buttons, one, two, three, four, five, making sure the buttonhole met the right button. Next, I pulled on my pants-called puddle jumpers because they were outgrown slacks that came up halfway to the calves of my legs. After putting on my ankle socks, I slipped my feet back into my slippers.

The slippers that looked like pink cotton candy from the circus when I received them on Christmas morning, six months later, looked like two scruffy abandoned dogs with tufts of matted fur. The slippers knew how to stay in step with the other slippers as they passed the talking mirrors that we looked into when we stood in line to get our hair brushed.

The matron faced us to the mirror and shamed us by saying, "Look at those buck teeth. You are getting fat. You are so skinny I can see your bones." Even when she wasn't there and I walked past the mirror, I heard her words coming from the reflection in the glass.

Just across from the talking mirror was the matron's private room. The slippers knew not to sneak into the matron's bedroom and snoop around like I wanted to do. After we had passed through the swinging doors into the long hallway, we passed a desk with a black rotary phone. As I marched down the hallway, the slippers knew not to run and slide down the shiny floors like I wanted to do.

When the matron was in her room with the door tightly shut, and I knew the coast was clear, I took off the slippers and slid down the long hallway floor, pretending I was Gretel, Hans Brinker's younger sister ice skating on a pond in Holland. The slippers knew the way to the dining room for breakfast.

After sitting at my assigned place at the table, I folded my hands and bowed my head for grace. "Thank you for the food we eat. Thank you for the birds that sing. Thank you, God, for everything. Amen."

I gulped down the cold glass of milk. When I tried to swallow the first bite of pasty cream of wheat, my stomach began to churn. It was the same feeling when I went around and around on the merry-go-round at the playground. The lumpy cereal got caught in my throat, and I began to gag.

"Don't you start this again, Jeanette. You know what will happen," the matron scolded. Even though I knew that the bowl of cereal would be sitting in front of me for lunch and again for supper, I still couldn't swallow.

I would wait for Valerie to sneak me a half of her peanut butter and jelly sandwich from lunch.

After breakfast, I took my fork, knife, spoon and empty milk glass to the kitchen. The bowl of cereal stayed on the placemat. It was my turn to wash dishes, so I put on a white apron that tied in the back and stood on a stepstool to reach the sink filled with hot sudsy water that turned my hands red. The girl next to me rinsed the dishes, and the girl next to her dried the dishes. A nice lady named Mrs. Hickman put the dishes away.

After our kitchen chores, the three of us walked back down the hallway and stopped at the cubby hall room to shine our shoes for church. I rubbed out the black scuff marks using a rag and Vaseline.

"Ring, Ring, Ring." I heard the black rotary phone ring.

And then I heard Valerie's voice. "Hello."

I thought, "OH NO!" Children are not allowed to answer or make calls on the telephone.

"Valerie, what do you think you are doing?"

"I was just answering the phone for you."

"You know the rules."

I peeked out from the doorway of the cubby hall room to see the matron grab Valerie's reddish, brown head of hair with her left hand and the phone handle with her right hand. The matron was hitting Valerie's head with the hard, plastic black handle. Valerie's glasses flew across the shiny floor. Valerie couldn't see without her glasses. Blood was running down the side of her face.

I wanted to run and help her, but instead I cowered in the corner of the cubby room and returned to rubbing the black scuff marks off the patent leather shoes. Next, I cleaned my everyday shoes; a brown pair of leather oxfords with Buster Brown and his dog at the bottom. The fumes of the shoe polish made me dizzy. I forgot about Valerie.

Instead, I thought about the day I got my Buster Brown shoes. It was after I was dispensed a pair of shoes from the Mooseheart shoe store that were a size to small and hurt my feet so bad that I couldn't walk. I was afraid to tell the matrons because she would call me a cry-baby. When the shoes rubbed blisters on my feet, and I couldn't walk anymore, the matron sent me to the dispensary.

After the doctor saw how bad my feet were, he put sticky mole skin on the blisters and said: "You are only allowed to wear slippers until your feet heal." I told him the matron would be mad if I only wore slippers and he said he would take care of it. "Nurse Bailey, write this little girl a note that she is not to wear shoes until her feet heal."

Thankfully, it was summer, and I was allowed to wear my slippers outside if it wasn't raining. Within a week, the guard took me to a real shoe store in Chicago, where they measured my feet to make sure I had the right size shoe. I was fitted with a pair of Red Ball Jet sneakers for play, a brown pair of oxfords for school and a pair of shiny patent leather shoes for church. The latter two pair of shoes had a little boy named Buster Brown winking his eye with a dog on the inside sole.

I felt quite special for the next year until I outgrew the shoes and was dispensed with a black and white pair of ill-fitting saddle shoes. My mom complained to Mr. Ketz, the superintendent, and he told her that the trip to the shoe store in Chicago was a one- time thing and from now on if I needed special shoes, she would have to pay for them. She told me, "I can't afford to buy you expensive shoes from Chicago, but I'll take you to Aurora to buy you a pair of Keds from the five and dime store."

After our shoes had been polished, it was time for chores. I wished I had the chore of tying rags on my feet and skating across the waxed marble floors so that I could go ice skating again, but this month my Saturday chore was to scrub down the wood steps that led to the basement. The Matron set two, one-gallon, stainless steel bean buckets at the top of the steps. One was filled with a mixture of ammonia and vinegar and the other plain water. I got a wash rag, a rinse rag and a dry rag from the rag bag.

Pictures of Valerie keep coming back into my mind, but I tried not to think of her as I dipped the first rag into the into the hot sudsy water. I tried to hold my breath because the strong ammonia smell burnt my nostrils. Twenty times, I wrung the rag out as tight as I could and washed each step, then I rinsed each step, then I dried each step until I reached the basement where one of the Mooseheart moms lived.

Mrs. Fowler had over ten children at Mooseheart and lived at Muncie Hall, where there was enough room for her children to visit her on Sunday afternoons. The fragrance of Avon Daisy perfume wafted from her room, and I called her Mrs. Flower because her room smelled so good.

The door to her room was slightly ajar, so I peeked into her room. She opened the door and waved me into her room to sit on the sofa. Her hands shook as she opened a box of graham crackers and offered me one. After gobbling down the graham cracker, I quickly emptied the scrub buckets into the basement sink and hung the rags up on the clothesline in the boiler room.

SLAM! The door to the boiler room shut. I tried to find my way to the door in the dark, but it wouldn't open. One of the other girls thought it was funny to shut me in the dark room. I bit my bottom lip and sat in the corner and cried until she decided to open the door and then called me a cry baby.

After morning chores, it was time for lunch; there was an empty seat at my table. Valerie wasn't there. There would be no peanut butter sandwich for me today. I drank my glass of milk and stared at the oatmeal. The matron lectured us about using the phone and not following the rules.

She didn't tell us, but I knew Valerie was taken to the dispensary by the watchman who drove around the orphanage in a station wagon with brown wood panels on the side. When we were sick or hurt, he picked up kids at the halls and dropped them off at the big concrete hospital with lots of windows.

After lunch on Saturday, the Catholic girls went to Catholic Education Classes to get ready for their First Holy Communion. While they were at church, the Protestant girls sat with our feet under the dressers on the cold, hard tile floor.

If we wiggled, the matron, who reminded me of the Wicked Witch of the West, put one of her hands over our mouth and the other on the back of our head and shook us back and forth yelling, "I'll shake you like a dog shakes a rabbit. You, protestant girls are just a bunch of heathens and will burn in hell someday."

When the Catholic girls came back to the hall, wearing pretty white hankies on their heads they bragged about their First Holy Communion. To compensate, I imagined I was Catholic and came up with the name Anna as my saint name.

On Saturday afternoons, I didn't visit my mom at Loyalty Hall because that was her day off. In the afternoon, I played outside on the playground, across from Muncie Hall. Debbie Lehman, Kathy Brasch, Peggy Davis and I ran towards the swing set calling dibs on the swings. There were only three swings and just like when we played musical chairs, one of us was left out. Peggy walked slowly to the merry-go-round.

While I was swinging back and forth, trying to touch the clouds with my red ball jet sneakers I spotted a lady and a man holding hands in the distance, walking towards the playground together; I recognized my mom, dressed in a flowered, cotton, button down dress with a belt at the waist. She was waving at me.

As the two of them got closer, I wondered who the man was; I recognized him as 'Uncle Leo,' the man that helped get us to Mooseheart. After my daddy had died, 'Uncle Leo' brought us food and took my mommy places. He even drove her out to Mooseheart so she could see where we would be living. When we boarded the train in Pennsylvania, he kissed her and then patted her butt, leaving his hand there for a long time.

I pretended not to see them as I jumped off the swings and scrambled up the ladder of a red caboose that sat on the lone railway track. A Moose Club donated the caboose to the playground. Inside the caboose, Tammy Ruple was pretending she was running away from Mooseheart. I climbed the iron ladder steps, and when I reached the black mesh platform, Tammy asked for my ticket. When I handed her a pretend ticket, she said, "All aboard!" I heaved my pretend luggage onto a shelf, and we sat down together on a cushioned seat and made believe we were leaving Mooseheart.

My dream was shattered when the couple found me in the caboose. "Jeanette, say hello to Uncle Leo. We got a special permit for you to visit with us today." I climbed down the ladder, turning to wave goodbye to Tammy.

I followed my mom over to an old beat up car that I didn't recognize. Uncle Leo opened the back door and said, "Hop in." My sister Ginny sat in the front. She scooted over, and my mom sat next to her. 'Uncle Leo' got in the driver's seat and turned the key to start the motor. Fumes of black smoke spilled out of the back of the car. He lit up a Camel cigarette with the push-in lighter and sent puffs of smoke swirling through the car, making it hard for me to breath. After shifting the car into gear, my mom told him when to turn to pick up my brothers at their halls. He could only find two of them on the campus, and they piled in the back seat with me crammed in the middle.

My mom directed 'Uncle Leo' down to the lake to go fishing and have a picnic. When we got out of the car 'Uncle Leo' opened the large trunk of the car and took out a couple of bamboo fishing poles. After giving the boys their poles and putting worms on the end of the hooks, he gave me a pretty bride doll wrapped in clear plastic paper.

"I bought his for my little bride girl." The paper crinkled as I tore it off trying to get to the bride doll. I wanted to feel the pretty white dress and her silky blonde hair. She smelled brand new.

'Uncle Leo' knelt down and stared into my eyes. "She's as pretty as you are. Let's take a walk over to see the water."

My brothers were busy with their fishing poles. My mother was sitting at a picnic table drinking a can of beer--which I didn't think she was supposed to be doing—watching the boys casting their lines into the water. Pretty soon I couldn't see them anymore through the tall grass surrounding the lake. And they couln't see me or 'Uncle Leo.' He found a place to sit on the ground and motioned for me to sit on his lap. "Would you like to be my little bride girl?" he asked as he unbuttoned my blouse and pulled down my slacks. "This is our secret. Don't ever tell anyone else."

At supper, that night Valerie was in her chair with a white bandage around the top of her head. She was quiet and didn't even say grace with us. I gulped down my milk and stared at the bowl of cereal, while the other girls ate chicken, mashed potatoes, and canned corn.

After supper, it was time for our Sunday night bath. When I got undressed, the matron noticed a rash on my bottom and red in my underpants. She questioned what I had been doing to myself. I didn't know what she was talking about. The hot soapy water burnt my chaffed skin.

After our bath on Saturday night, dressed in our pajamas and slippers, we walked to the living room where we sat crossed legged on the shiny floor and watched *The Lawrence Welk Show*. I liked watching the bubbles float up in the air behind the bandstand. We all wanted to sit by Valerie because she was hurt. Valerie liked The Lennon Sisters and told us that her sister Janet could sing better than Janet Lennon. Kathy Brasch and Peggy Davis bragged because they had the same names as the other sisters.

At night, a different matron came to put us to bed. In a Southern drawl sang *This Little Light of Mine* before we went to bed. We turned the sheet and blanket down and crawled into our beds with stiff white sheets and a scratchy blanket. I wondered where the light that she sang about was, because all I felt was darkness. In the morning, we made our beds and again put our pajamas under the pillow to wear the next night.

On Sunday mornings, instead of wearing our play clothes we dressed for church in our white slips, scratchy dresses, white, lacy ankle socks and shiny patent leather shoes without black scuffs. After we were dressed we waited for the church bells of the world's largest 110-foot bell tower to chime throughout the campus, telling us it's time for church. The matron lined us up, two by two and we walked to the church called the House of God.

The children's cathedral, built in the 1940's was a large stone building in the shape of a cross with a Protestant sanctuary flanking the left side and a Catholic sanctuary flanking the right side. In the main sanctuary, there were two aisles of seats.

During the Church services, I sat with my mother and five older brothers on the left side in the fifth wooden pew from the front. My little friends that didn't have a mommy or daddy sat with the matron on the right-hand side. My older sister wore a burgundy gown with a gold sash like the rest of the older girls who sat behind the altar and sing in the choir.

'Uncle Leo' came to church and sat by my mother. When the organ began to play *The Old Rugged Cross,* the both sang together. While everyone was standing, I went to the end of the pew and sat as far away as I could from the creepy guy that sat next to my mom.

Reverend Hamrick, who I called Mr. Hammerhead preached, "Cast your bread upon the waters, and they will come back to you." During the preaching, I got bored and rummaged through my mother's white plastic handbag to find her and my dad's black and white wedding picture. She was young and pretty, and wore a string of pearls. He was clean shaven and handsome, wearing a white shirt and tie.

After the sermon, a large gold plate lined with a burgundy cloth at the bottom was passed around. Everyone deposited an envelope with a penny in the plate. In the summer, when Moose members visited for the large conventions, they attended church services. This was the fiftieth anniversary of Mooseheart, so the church was filled with people. The offering plate that was passed around overflowed with cash bills. I lived up to my name as a heathen and slipped a few of the dollars into my pocket.

After church, my mom took me to the fieldhouse to see Ginny graduate with the class of 1963. Crowds and crowds of people were there for the fiftieth anniversary celebration of Mooseheart. Whenever I was with lots people, I felt like I couldn't breathe. After the ceremony, my sister left on a train. 'Uncle Leo' departed the same day, and thankfully we never saw or heard from him again.

On Monday, I was called to the dispensary; the doctor and the nurse checked my bottom. They said I must be allergic to rag weed. Nurse Bailey soaked a cotton ball in pink Calamine Lotion and rubbed it all over my bottom and the itching stopped. The nurse asked me if anyone touched me down there. My face turned red and I shook my head no.

While living at Muncie Hall, I met new girls who were a year older than me. Mimi Maly and I both were from Pennsylvania which made us instant friends. Mimi's older sister Karen visited Mimi on Tuesdays. That was the one day a week when older siblings could visit their younger siblings. Only girls could visit their sisters while the boys could visit their brothers. Karen was so pretty with her long blonde hair and always made us laugh. She would read Mimi letters from Troy, Pennsylvania. The writing was in large print that looked like a little child's writing.

I asked Mimi who the letters were from and when she told me her mom, I didn't believe her. I couldn't understand why an adult would write like a child. If she had a mom, she would be here at Mooseheart, like my mom, along with all the other kids who had moms.

Years later, after I moved back to Pennsylvania, a friend and I were driving to the eastern part of the state via Route 6 and drove through Troy, Pa. When I saw the facility that was the return address on the envelopes from Mimi's mom, a flood of memories rushed into my head. Mimi wasn't lying to me. I assumed Mimi's mom was mentally ill and couldn't take care of her.

A few years later, when I first got a computer I found Mimi's sister Karen, who was living in West Virginia. We met in Seven Springs, Pa for a Mother Earth Convention and I asked her about her mom. She told me her mom wasn't mentally ill but had had a stroke. After the stroke, the family went to Mooseheart and her mom wasn't allowed to see her children again until they were eighteen and left Mooseheart when they graduated. With therapy, her mom recovered and went back to college for a degree. The bond with her children had been severed.

Even though Mimi was a year older than me, she was a lot smaller. She had pretty blonde hair like her sister. One day, Mimi just disappeared. I assumed she left Mooseheart like other kids sometimes did. When kids left, no one told us why and we never said good-bye or heard from them again. I was heartbroken when Mimi left and didn't come back. When she returned to the hall after being away for a few months, I was delighted.

At bedtime, while we were getting ready for bed, Mimi took off her shirt to put her pajamas on and I saw a big scar on her chest.

"Mimi, what happened to you?"

She whispered, "I had a hole in my heart, the doctors fixed it at the Children's Hospital in Chicago." While Mimi was in the hospital, a doctor wanted to adopt her, but the authorities at Mooseheart wouldn't let her be adopted. Mimi had three older sisters, and they said that it was more important to keep the family together

Mimi wasn't allowed to go outside to play, so I stayed inside with her for afternoon playtime. We were allowed to play in the little play area with child-sized tables, a kitchen set, and some puzzles, as long as we didn't make a mess. Everything had to stay in it's place, so we played very carefully until she was well enough to go outside to play.

In the summer, a big truck dropped off bicycles at the halls. There were only five bikes for ten kids. The bikes didn't have training wheels and there wasn't anyone to teach us how to ride, so we were on our own.

I called dibs on a little red rusty bike. I could touch the sidewalk with my tippy toes and walked the bike on the sidewalk to master the steering. Then I discovered that the bike coasted when it was on downhill grade. I balanced the bike and lifted my feet as the bike moved faster and faster. It didn't take long for me to figure out how to pedal the bike. I loved the wind blowing in my hair and the feeling of being independent and free.

For my birthday that year, my mother bought me a new Schwinn blue bike with a banana seat and high handlebars, which I wouldn't share with anyone.

We were allowed to ride our bikes to Georgia-Alabama Hall, which was a boys Hall next to Muncie Hall. The boys rode their bikes up to Muncie Hall and back until one of them wrecked his bike. I ran over to see if he was okay and was terrified to see his leg stuck in the spokes, with a bone visible. I looked up to see a matron in a checkered, cotton dress as she screamed, "You kids leave him alone!"

When she saw the hurt little boy, in ten decibels higher she screamed, "You little daredevil; I told you to slow down on that bike. You kids get back to your hall this very minute." A watchman in the large brown station wagon showed up to take the little boy to the hospital.

On Sunday afternoons, we went to the football field for Drum and Bugle Corp concerts. As part of the ROTC military program, along with other boys dressed up in army uniforms and marched on the field to patriotic music. After the program, candy was scattered on the football field by someone dressed in a clown costume. All of the younger children gathered up the treats to the tune of a song called *The Candy Man*, that blared through the squeaking loudspeakers. We stuffed our mouths with as much candy as possible before we went back to the hall.

I was sick a lot while I lived in Muncie Hall. When I swallowed my throat hurt and my bottom lip had a perpetual fever blister that wouldn't go away. After I turned six years old in August, I had my tonsils taken out. The nurses, Mrs. Bailey, and Mrs. Brasch were so nice to me, but when I saw Dr. Hellman, I got the shivers and wanted to run away. The doctor was tall with black hair and wore black plastic glasses. After getting my tonsils out, all I could eat for the next week was hot salty broth and red Jello.

When I returned to the hall, I didn't have an appetite. The matrons tried to force me to eat, but the sight of food made me gag. I was so skinny that the other children start calling me Twiggy after the famous model who was very thin and had short hair, just like me. Sometimes I would wake up in the middle of night vomiting and while still dressed in my pajamas, the watchman that took the little boy that broke his leg to the hospital, came and took me to the hospital in the big brown station wagon. Child abuse clearances were unheard of, and there was never another person with the watchman when he took us to the hospital at night.

While recovering from the tonsillectomy, I came down with the mumps and was sent back to the hospital. While there, my mom visited me once for a few minutes, but I didn't know what to say to her, and I felt embarrassed because I was sick. She seemed like a stranger to me.

I preferred being sick and spending time at the hospital where the nurses were kind and never scolded me. We watched television most of the day and were treated to vanilla ice cream at night.

A nice priest visited in the evenings and sometimes played card games with me. When I saw the black shirt and pants walking up the hallway, I would line up all the cards in numerical order and asked him if he wanted to play a game of concentration with me. He always agreed and I always won the game.

When I didn't get well, the watchman took me to a hospital outside of Mooseheart where I was diagnosed as a "failure to thrive child." Each morning the matron slathered a tablespoon of yellow, sticky stuff called Vi-Daylin on top of my cereal.

At Christmas time, there was a pretty tree decorated in the living room of Muncie Hall. The day before Christmas a tall pine tree in front of the House of God was ceremoniously lit up by Moose Members. On Christmas Eve, all the kids at Mooseheart walked to the church for an evening service and Christmas hymns, ending with everyone singing *Silent Night.* As we walked back to our halls in the dark, with sparkling snow falling on our faces, I imagined magic was sprinkling down from the night sky.

When we returned to the hall, Santa came for a visit, and each of us received an orange and a candy cane. I knew a man was dressed up as Santa because my older brothers told me Santa Claus wasn't real. They told me if I didn't believe them, to just pull on his beard and see what happened. I did just that when we were together for a family photo that would be sent to the Moose Club. Not only was Santa not real; he was a little too friendly with his hands when I sat on his lap.

Santa left each child a gift under the tree and in the morning, we opened the presents. Moose members were generous at Christmas, although the toys we received were immediately packed away in a closet that was off limits to the children. Our new underwear and socks were sent to the laundry to be labeled with our laundry number.

For Christmas dinner, we were assigned to one of our siblings' halls for a big meal with our family. After the meal, we went to visit our mom at Loyalty Hall. My mom had asked me what I wanted for Christmas, and there were only two things. The first thing was what I wanted every year. I wanted my daddy. I liked the popular song *How Much is that Doggie in the Window* and if I couldn't have a real dog, the second thing I wanted was a stuffed puppy dog.

I never got my daddy back, but my brother Paul saved enough money from doing chores at Mooseheart to buy me a large stuffed dog that was as big as I was. When I took the toy back to Muncie Hall, all the kids wanted to play with it, so the matron took it away and I never saw it again.

The Saturday before Easter, a member of a local Moose Club dressed up as the Easter Bunny with a big head. I felt creeped out by eyes staring at me through the mask. I was glad that I didn't have to sit on the Easter Bunny's lap. The Moose members filled our baskets with candy but the matrons confiscated it when we returned to the hall.

Every Easter, we were dispensed with a new dress, hat, socks, and patent leather shoes that would be our Sunday shoes for the year. Early on Sunday morning, we walked hand in hand together to the House of God to celebrate Easter. After the service, we went to one of our siblings' assigned halls for ham, sweet potatoes, mashed potatoes and canned green beans. My appetite had returned, and I began to gain some weight.

In spring, when the blossoms appeared on the trees and the grass began to turn green and birds chirped in the morning, I began to find comfort in nature. The grounds of the campus came alive with colorful pansies, petunias and gladiolas blooming that bordered large concrete water fountains and structures. Even Parker, the spray truck returned to spray trees. Nature was the one thing I could count on that wasn't harmful to me. Although the sun disappeared behind the clouds, it always returned.

I lived at Muncie Hall for two years. On my sixth birthday, a brown paper package from Pennsylvania arrived in the mail. Scribbled in the corner were the words Elizabeth Van Zanten. It was a package from my Dutch Oma! When I tore off the paper and opened the box, a familiar aroma of camphor and cloves transported me back in time. I was delighted to find a tin of Oma's Speculaas cookies, a package of black licorice, a red umbrella and a pair of red galoshes. I shared the cookies and licorice with my friends. They gobbled down the cookies, but turned their noses up at the salty black licorice. I was happy to have it all to myself.

The first day it rained after receiving the package, I pulled on my red galoshes that I had to tug to get over my saddle shoes. The matron wouldn't allow me to open the umbrella in the hall and I was anxious to use it. When I stepped outside there was a slight breeze with a drizzle of rain falling from the cloudy sky. As I opened the umbrella a huge gust of wind came along and took me along with it. Rather than feeling frightened when my feet lifted off the ground, I found myself feeling free and light and imagined what it would be like to be like a bird and fly high above the clouds.

The wind swept me to and fro to a place of beauty and magic, something like the Lollipop Land from the Wizard of Oz, except more heavenly. There were flying horses, angelic beings, rainbows of light shining in all directions and vibrations of sound that were more beautiful than anything I had ever heard.

I looked down and saw the darkness of Mooseheart underneath me and thought of all my friends. In a flash my feet returned to the concrete sidewalk and the gentle rain turned into a thunderstorm. I bolted back into the hall and shook the rain off the umbrella before I went back in the hall. When I took my galoshes off, I looked up to see the stern face of the matron, with hands on her hips, her arms crossed and a deep wrinkle in her brow. She grabbed the umbrella and scoldingly asked what I thought I was doing, going outside without permission. Without giving me time to answer, she threw the umbrella in the trash can and ordered me to stand in the corner until further notice. Although she took away the umbrella she wasn't able to take away my imagination.

Although there were fences all around me, I felt as if I was going to survive this experience and find freedom. Years later, I came across a poem titled "On a Sunny Evening" by an anonymous writer in 1944, that described how I felt about this time in my life.

The sun has made a veil of gold

So lovely that my body aches.

Above, the heavens shriek with blue.

Convinced, I've smiled by some mistake.

The world's abloom and seems to smile.

I want to fly but where, how high?

If in a barbed wire, things can bloom

Why couldn't I. I will not die!

Chapter Four

I don't remember one child crying a tear on the first day of school at Mooseheart. Instead of missing our parents, we were happy to be away from the matrons. Kindergarten class was in the basement of Muncie Hall. The Matron didn't want to hear any clomping from our saddle shoes, so we tiptoed carefully down the shiny wood steps. We stood single file, the girls in one line and the boys in the other, waiting for the teacher to unlock the door to the classroom.

When Mrs. Springer, a short, stout woman with curly hair and a cotton dress that buttoned up the front, opened the doors, we marched into the classroom like little soldiers. Before we took our seats, we faced the red, white and blue American flag and recited the Pledge of Allegiance.

Mrs. Springer passed out books with a picture of a little boy with black hair dressed in shorts and a striped shirt playing with a little girl with curly blonde hair.

On the chalkboard, she made lines with three pieces of chalk attached to a wooden handle that squeaked as she pulled it across the board. With a single piece of chalk, she printed the letters D-I-C-K. "Now class everyone says DICK."

We all repeated after her. She did the same with the words JANE, SALLY, SPOT, and PUFF. Then we took turns reading the words from the book. I couldn't turn the pages fast enough to find out what happened next in the story.

Math didn't come as easy, so I counted on my fingers. At free time, we played with playdough. The smell made me nauseous but it was fun squishing it through my fingers. Unlike the matron, Mrs. Springer let us make messes and commended us for cleaning up without being told. With a little practice and the help of my friend Debbie Lehman, I learned to skip to the song *Skip to My Lou* playing on the phonograph that went around and around in circles.

On November 22, 1963, we entered a dark classroom with the lights turned off. After we had said the Pledge of the Allegiance, we sat down crossed leg on the floor and watched a parade on the black and white television. It wasn't a parade of clowns and bands playing instruments. People riding in black cars were dressed in black clothes.

Mrs. Springer explained the funeral of the president, John F. Kennedy. His daughter, Caroline was three when her daddy died, the same age I was when my daddy died. I wanted to cry, but looked around at the other children and didn't see any tears, so I swallowed mine.

Mrs. Naden, my first-grade teacher, was a thin lady with purple hair and never smiled. When I couldn't make my K's correctly, she put clothes pins on my ears and made me stand out in the hallway. Eventually, I learned how to print perfectly so that she wouldn't put clothespins on my ears ever again.

My friend, Tammy Ruple, sat in the front row and Mrs. Naden hollered at her a lot. When Tammy didn't listen, Mrs. Naden drew a circle on the chalkboard and made Tammy stand with her nose inside of the circle. If she wiggled or squirmed Mrs. Naden slapped her bare legs with a wooden ruler. The rest of us knew to behave.

I moved to Seattle Hall when I was eight years old and got a new, used bed and new, used drawers. Mrs. Silvas was the new, used matron. A new girl from Oregon moved into our hall. Her name was Barbara and she had curly red hair and freckles and was shy and quiet. She seemed scared, so I helped her out when she didn't know what the rules were.

I liked making new friends and helping people. Sometimes new girls would come but would only stay a week or so and then leave. They said their mom or dad was coming to get them.

Sometimes they did and sometimes they didn't. At school, I liked learning about different states in geography class so I could find out where different kids came from. When I looked on the map in Geography class and found out how far away Oregon was, I felt sorry for Barbara and tried to be extra nice to her.

On Saturdays, we went to the auditorium to see movies. Sometimes they were cowboy and Indian movies. Sometimes the movies were about little girls that were kidnapped and taken into the woods and killed. The matrons showed us newspaper articles from the Chicago Tribune newspaper about little girls who were abducted and told us that's what would happen to us if we ever tried to run away from Mooseheart.

On Sundays, we attended concerts and programs in a large auditorium. All the Mooseheart students, except for the preschoolers, were required to attend. My five brothers always complained about having to go to the stupid concert, but for me, the orchestra music sounded beautiful. One of the programs was a man who made beautiful things out of glass that he heated and then blew into shapes. Jerry Lewis came to perform and made everyone laugh.

During the summer, we were allowed more freedom to go on hikes and go fishing at the Mooseheart Lake. We used bamboo rods donated by Moose Clubs. Summer counselors helped us put worms on the hooks and attach a red and white bobber. Every once in a while, one of us would catch a sunfish or bluegill that we released back into the water.

The lake had a little house for boats. Sometimes we were allowed to paddle the boats around the lake. On the fourth of July, we dressed in long pants and sweaters and walked down to the lake to watch the fireworks at night. It was one of the only times we were allowed to be outside at night.

Now that I was getting older, I could walk by myself to the dentist, to the beauty shop to get my hair cut and to see my mother. I had to carry a permit with my destination stating the exact time I would be back, not a minute later.

Daily visits to my mom were difficult. The transition from being with my friends to seeing her for an hour a day, then going back to the hall confused me. On Sundays, all five of us kids visited her at one time in a small room. Sometimes it wasn't all five because my older brothers Paul and Bill would be at the detention farm for getting in trouble.

My brothers teased and picked on me a lot until they made me cry. When my mom told them to stop, they began calling me "Brat." When things got out of control, she would take us for a ride around the lake in a Rambler that she traded for the green 1957 station wagon. The nickname "Brat" stuck and it would be many years before I heard any of my brothers call me Jeanette again.

To avoid the frustration of my brothers, I started visiting a lady that lived across the hall from my mom. Mrs. Hunden was a heavy-set woman, with curly red hair who sweated profusely. When I visited her, she would be sitting on the couch knitting, dressed in a sleeveless cotton dress covered with a white apron. I asked her if she would teach me how to knit. She gave me two wooden pointed sticks and some yarn and taught me how to cast on stitches and knit. I started to look forward to visiting my mom so that I could see Mrs. Hunden.

My mom and other mothers gathered in the kitchen of Loyalty Hall for coffee while the kids ran around and played. Unsupervised, we went outside and flew kites in the spring, built snow chairs in the winter and sometimes played in real cars with keys still in the ignition. One day my brother Warren started the green station wagon, put it in gear and started driving. He was only ten, and I was eight. I knew he didn't know what he was doing and started screaming and crying for help. He slammed on the breaks and said: "Maybe we shouldn't be driving this car."

My mom worked in different halls cooking for the older boys. When I visited her after school during the week for one hour I had to find out where she was working. Not only was she in a different place each time, but I started to notice that she acted differently. I thought I had two mothers. One was happy and laughing and knew my name. The other one was depressed and didn't seem to recognize me.

With a special yellow permit, parents or guardians were given permission to take us outside of Mooseheart for a few hours. Sometimes on Sundays, we went to the "forest preserve" for picnics. My dad's friend Fred from Pennsylvania came out to visit, and now he was kissing and holding my mom's hand. I wondered how my daddy would have felt about that. He talked a lot about how pretty Pennsylvania was compared to Illinois and told me there were so many trees that they didn't need to have forest preserves. The whole state was a forest. When he talked about Pennsylvania, I felt sad to be so far away from where I was born.

On weekend visits, my mom took us to a man's apartment in St. Charles. There were twenty wooden steps to his apartment with a living room, couch and chair, a small kitchen with a little stove and fridge. My mom and the man would go into the bedroom while my brother Warren and I watched cartoons on a small black and white television.

The man's name was Arnie. He had a big fat belly, wore a white shirt and breathed very heavily. Arnie kissed my mom and held her hand. I was afraid he might become my daddy. I didn't like him, and he didn't like me. The only reason he was nice to me was because he liked my mom.

Sometimes Arnie and my mom took my brothers and me places outside of Mooseheart. Unlike the whole orphans, I had tastes of freedom when they took us to visit a real windmill at Fabian Park near Aurora, an animal park where we could pet and feed deer, an orchard to pick apples and out to eat at a nice restaurant called The Fisherman's Inn in Elburn.

We had picnics at a park and waded in the Fox River and went Go-Kart racing. I was too little to drive, so my brother Paul let me sit on his lap and drove me around the black paved track. Other times, when there was just Warren and me, they took us to a local Moose Club so they could drink while we sat and did nothing.

A memorable trip outside Mooseheart was when my mom and her friend, Mrs. Stucky, took me to see *Sound of Music* at a real theater in Aurora. The sound of the music filled the theater, and I was mesmerized by the voice of Julie Andrews and dreamed that someday I would have a father like Mr. Von Trapp. I was particularly interested in how the family escaped the Nazi regime and thought about how I could escape from Mooseheart someday.

There were occasions when I left the confines of Mooseheart without my mom. At least once a year for a field trip, we boarded a school bus that all the kids called the Kidney Shaker. Marvin Robey, a heavy-set man who wore the same color pants and shirt, drove us to Naperville, Illinois for live theater productions, sponsored by Moose Clubs.

In the wintertime when our hall won a Christmas decorating contest, we went to a roller-skating rink, out to eat at a Big Boy Restaurant and then for a tour of the city Christmas lights.

In the summer, we went to the circus. I always got sick from the fumes of the bus and didn't particularly care to see animals in cages and jumping through hoops at the crack of a whip. It felt all too familiar.

After first grade, elementary school was better, and school was an escape from the structure and rigidity of the halls. The teachers were much nicer than the matrons. I figured it was because they didn't have to live at Mooseheart. Mrs. Thee taught Geography and gave me an A for the map I drew of Illinois, although she accused me of tracing. We had religion class and learned about the stories in the Old Testament from a retired Army

Chaplain. I thought about how God parted the Red Sea for Moses and wondered if someday He could get me out of Mooseheart.

Mrs. Klussendorf taught Science and was extra kind to me. Her husband managed the dairy farm where my brothers spent a lot of time and she seemed to know who I was. There was a question on a test that asked how much energy it would take for a boy to move a house that weighed one hundred and fifty pounds. I wrote zero because a house weighed more than 150 pounds and a boy could never move it. I thought I was a smart ass, but she gave me an A on the test for such a brilliant answer.

In music class, we learned how to sing folk songs and musicals. When we sang the song *Five Hundred Miles* I felt lost, and tears welled up in my eyes. I felt so far away from home. Each year we were introduced to musicals and did a musical performance. The year we performed *Mary Poppins* we were allowed to watch the movie in class. Mary Poppins reminded me of the experience with the red umbrella and I was glad to know I wasn't alone in my ability to create imaginative experiences. I fell in love with the lyrical music of *Supercalifragilisticexpialidocious* and *Chim Chim Che-ree.* I wondered why we couldn't draw with chalk on all the sidewalks throughout the campus. We also took field trips to a theater in Naperville to see live performances. I loved being transported to places of imagination and magic.

In reading class, the teacher read us *Little House on The Prairie* by Laura Ingalls Wilder. My favorite character was the mother Caroline because she was sweet and kind to Laura. I imagined that I, had a mother like her and while walking back to the hall after school, I felt her holding my hand and talking to me. I tried to imagine that the matron's name was Caroline, but it didn't change her personality.

The class I liked best was library because there were more books than I could count. When I found a collection of Oz books by Frank Baum and read the whole series, I was again reminded of my Uncle Henry and Aunt Velma and wondered if they were still alive. Each day that I walked the long walk to school from the hall, I pretended the sidewalk was the yellow brick road, and that school was the land of Oz.

In 1966, my brothers Paul and Bill graduated from Mooseheart. My Aunt Velma, Aunt Leota and other relatives traveled from Pennsylvania for the ceremony. I was happy to know they were still alive. They stayed at a place called the Tic Toc Motel outside of Mooseheart.

My mom never spoke highly of her sisters and said that they, particularly Aunt Velma, were uppity-and they were compared to my mom. They wore make-up and lipstick, and their shiny brunette hair was always tightly curled. Their clothes were always neatly pressed, and they wore cardigans and had purses to match. My mom's clothes were always wrinkled, and she never wore make-up. She did get her hair done on special occasions and looked pretty when she was dressed up, but that wasn't often. The good thing was she didn't seem as stiff as her sisters.

After the boy's graduation, Bill stayed around the Aurora area for a while and then got a job at a dairy farm in Brookville, Pennsylvania. Paul went to Bailey's Technical Institute in St. Louis and then landed a well-paying job in Rockford, Illinois. He started dating a high school classmate, Dottie Spohn, who also graduated from Mooseheart and attended the St. Anthony College of Nursing in Rockford.

I moved to Virginia Hall when I was nine years old. Some of the girls living in the hall were a year older than me. There were two separate wings for bedrooms with ten beds lined in two rows, separated by closets at the bottom of the beds.

At night after getting our baths and pajamas on, we crawled into bed without saying prayers. There weren't curtains on the windows, and when the moon was full, it was as bright as day, making it hard to sleep. My friends and I stayed up talking and giggling until the matron came in and made us get out of bed, go into the living room, roll up the carpets and using old toothbrushes, we scrubbed the floors on our hands and knees until it was morning. Tornado warnings were frequent at Mooseheart.

When the whistle blew in the middle of the night we were herded down to the dank basement where we spent the night.

After Paul graduated he came back to take me to see the movie Born Free at the theater in Aurora. I fell in love with the orphaned lioness, Elsa and related to the feelings of her siblings being locked up. I was envious when Elsa was set free and hoped that someday I would be free. When we sang the song *Born Free* for a concert, I couldn't get the words out of my head. I dreamed of someday being free.

While I was moving from hall to hall each year, I lost track of what hall all my brothers were in, until my brother Jack moved to Maryland-Delaware Hall on the other side of Mooseheart.

My mom was assigned to cook in the hall while his houseparents, Mr.and Mrs. Gulley had a day off. The couple hailed from southern Illinois. When hired, they made it clear to the higher ups at Mooseheart that they would take care of any discipline needed for the boys. The boys wouldn't be sent to the farm-another name for the detention hall-for laborious hours of work such as digging pits for garbage and cleaning a house that was already spotless.

The Gulley's also found it atrocious that kids at Mooseheart were separated from their siblings and parents. The first time I met the couple was when our family was assigned to their hall for a Mother's Day dinner. All the kids that had moms who were living were given a red carnation to wear. If their mother died they wore a white carnation pinned to their dress or suit coat.

I had never met any of my brother's house parents and felt special going off girl's campus onto boy's campus to visit my older brother. The first time I walked in the back door of Maryland-Delaware hall, I had a real sense of a home. Granny, Mrs. Gulley's mother, a small framed woman, wearing an apron was stirring a batch of peanut butter fudge. Without knowing my name, she handed me a large wooden spoon with plenty of fudge still on it and said, "Sweetie, would you like to lick the spoon?"

Just as I was scraping the last of the candy off the spoon with my teeth, I felt another presence in the room. When I turned around, a tall woman with blonde hair styled in a beehive on top of her head was standing in the doorway. Expecting to get hollered at I stiffened up and hid the spoon behind my back.

Instead, I heard the kindest voice I ever heard say, "You must be Jack's little sister. I see that Van Zanten look in your eyes."

Rather than scolding me, she opened her arms and gave me the first hug I had in seven years. When she hugged me, I wanted to melt into her large bosoms, held up by a sturdy brassiere that I could see through her neatly pressed cotton blouse. "Charlie, look who we got here, Jack's little sister. Isn't she a cute one?"

Mr. Gulley came around the corner of the living room. The aroma of tobacco swirled around the house as he puffed on a pipe that he held between his strong jaw. He wore cowboy boots, blue jeans, a large belt buckle with an engraved horse and a long sleeve checkered shirt that had pearly white snaps instead of buttons. He had jet black hair, slicked neatly to the side. His deep, dark eyes didn't look away when he spoke.

"Well, hello young lady. It's a pleasure to meet you. We've heard a lot about you from your brother."

I hid behind Mrs. Gully and gave him a little wave.

I was surprised at the difference in Jack's behavior. There wasn't any teasing or monkey business. It seemed as if he had grown up into a respectable young man instead of an impish boy. He called me Brat only once while I was there.

Mrs. Gulley kindly reprimanded him "Don't you call her that."

"But that's what everyone calls her." He retorted.

"Her name is Jeanette, and that's what you will call her from now on." Mr. Gully chimed in, looking Jack directly in the eye. For a time, Jack didn't call me anything, but after a while he began to use my name.

My mom and Mrs. Gulley became good friends. When my mom made her annual pilgrimage back to Pennsylvania for funerals or vacations, I wouldn't tell my matron and would sneak over to see Mrs. Gulley for an hour visit. I pretended she was my mom.

While visiting her, I played with her little grandson Tommy Jo. He was just learning to walk, and I would hold his hands and walk him around the house while Mrs. Gulley and Granny prepared supper for the boys. On long Sunday afternoon visits when my mom was gone, Mrs. Gulley would get out her portable typewriter and help me to type a letter to her even though we didn't have an address for my mom.

When flowers were blossoming on the trees and the grass was turning green, a large truck delivered the bicycles that had been in storage for the winter, back to the halls. The chains were oiled, and flat tires were fixed. The bikes gave us the freedom to explore the large campus. My friends and I rode out to the real farm where there were horses and dairy cows.

Only the girls were permitted to ride the horses; the boys worked at the dairy farm taking care of the cows. An old man who we called Mr. Ed taught us how to clean the horse stalls and how to ride the horses. My first lesson was to mount the horse on the left-hand side.

Karen Maly always had dibs on the tall palomino horse named Charlie. I rode one of the quarter horses. We weren't supposed to canter the horses, but as soon as the barn was out of sight, we took off running. I don't know who liked it more, the horses or us. We relished in the feeling of complete freedom, with the wind blowing through our hair, as we cantered the horses around the lake.

During the summer, Moose members who attended the annual Moose convention, would flood Mooseheart to tour the campus. Select students were chosen as guides to give the visitors tours and the lucky few received generous tips.

Those of us who were more outspoken about how things were at Mooseheart weren't chosen to be guides, but we had fun getting money from the members by striking up a conversation with the visitors. After finding out what state they were from, we told them we were from the same state-even though we weren't-they gave us a five or ten-dollar bill that we kept to ourselves.

Each summer there were two things we could count on; one was moving to another hall, the other was going to Camp Ross in Mt. Morris, Illinois. The camp was seventy miles away from Mooseheart, and it was a pretty big deal getting on a bus and driving that far. Before going to camp, we got our annual tetanus shot and were issued military bags to pack enough clothes for a week.

The camp was a reprieve from the halls. We stayed in cabins that were reminiscent of military barracks with cots and trunks to store our clothes. Every morning we woke to the sound of a trumpet and were required to clean the cabin before breakfast. We walked a distance to the mess hall and then were kept busy with activities throughout the day, including long hikes to White Forest State Park and making arts and crafts.

College students, along with older teens from Mooseheart were counselors and didn't have insight into the needed safety for children. I nearly drowned at one of the pool relay races when we were required to swim in oversize sweatshirts and pants.

I wish I could say that this experience was fun, but it wasn't. The camp was managed by a man named Ritchie Bourdage. He spent a lot of time with boys at Mooseheart, introducing some of them to inappropriate sexual behavior. Older boys crept around the cabins at night, sometimes violating the girls.

The older girls who were our counselors acted like the matrons at the halls and were very strict. Each morning, the cabins were inspected and had to be spotless before we could head up to the mess hall for breakfast. In the evenings, we had skits, and I played the part of Puck from a Mid-Summer Night's Dream. I identified with the character, and that got me through two weeks of fear of boys coming into the cabins at night.

When I returned from camp that summer, my mother moved to Hart Hall, which was only a short distance from West Virginia Hall. During playtime my friends and I walked over to see her, and she would give us food. On my birthday, she had a party for me in the backyard and invited all of my friends. She put candles in a big watermelon slice and after I had blew them out, she cut each of us a piece of the juicy red fruit. When we had to go to the bathroom, because we weren't allowed in a different hall without a permit, she let us sneak in Hart Hall to use the toilet.

I was happy that she was in the same place every day and for the first time in her life, she seemed happy. She had a nice room that was more like a house than Loyalty Hall. Lilies of the Valley, my mom's favorite flower, blossomed next to the building.

For her birthday, on May 20th, Arnie gave her a beautiful ring with her emerald birthstone. I began to see glimpses of beauty in my mother. She started wearing prettier dresses and was so proud of a Christmas Cactus plant that blossomed with beautiful pink flowers. She seemed happy to be cooking for the other ladies that lived in the hall. I started helping my mom cook the meals. My favorite part was opening packages of Oscar Meyer hot dogs and getting a free piece of Bazooka Bubble Gum and then reading the comic inside of the wrapper.

Mrs. Meade, a seamstress, also lived in Hart Hall and made me dresses out of leftover corduroy fabric. When my brownie dress was too big, she took it in and hemmed it for me. When the boys came to Hart Hall to visit, they couldn't refrain from teasing me, and things often got out of hand. Our mom would shoo us all outside because the other ladies complained about our behavior.

During the day, the matron sent us outside to play and locked the door so that we couldn't get back in the hall, I was able to go to Hart Hall to visit my mom. I learned how to roller skate with a pair of silver skates that attached to my saddle shoes and that I tightened with a key. I tied a yellow piece of yarn on the key and wore it around my neck so I wouldn't lose it.

While playing outside in the spring, we found birds dying on the ground from the annual spray truck. We would sneak shoe boxes out of the hall and have funerals for the birds. When someone in our family died, we weren't allowed to leave Mooseheart to attend the funeral, so burying the birds was a way to grieve our losses.

After the funerals, a few of us Protestant girls snuck into the church to play in the Catholic confessionals. If there were any candles lit, we blew them out and slipped out the side door. We were caught once by a Catholic priest who had a boy in his office with him. When we saw each other, his face was redder than an apple. He scared the hell out of us and told us never to come back. We thought for sure we'd be in hot water after that, but we never got called to the dean's office.

At the end of summer, as the days got shorter, playing outdoors lasted into chilly, fall evenings. Ruby Gilson and Gaye York, who were a year older than me, gave me their sweaters when I was cold and shivering. We played jacks, hula hoop and rode our bikes. In the Autumn we raked up leaves to jump in and formed them into an outline of a house where we each had our very own bedroom.

When we ran out of things to do we gathered up twigs and started a fire to keep warm. We tried to get the fire so big that it would burn Mooseheart down, but the cold Chicago winds from Lake Michigan blew out the flames. We were happy when the loud supper time whistle blew, and we were allowed back in the hall to warm up and eat.

I didn't realize it then, but the feelings of grief from losing my father and early home, were beginning to thaw. It was only the tip of a huge ice-berg that would take many years to melt completely. Burying and having funerals for the dead birds was our way of processing this grief.

As an adult, I started collecting children's books on grief after reading *The Tenth Good Thing About Barney* by Judith Viorist to a group of preschool children at Head Start. Tears welled up in my eyes and my voice crackled as I read the book, wishing that someone would have read a story like this to me when I lost my daddy.

Chapter Five

In June of 1968, I packed my few belongings in a cardboard box and moved to East Legion Hall, located on the edge of the girl's campus that bordered the property line of Mooseheart. From the upstairs window of the hall, my friends and I could see the chain link fencing that contained us.

During our free time outdoors, we would sneak across the road to explore an abandoned ornamental concrete factory, where we discovered a railroad trestle that was off limits physically but not to my mind. I thought about Dorothy from the Wizard of Oz singing *Somewhere Over the Rainbow* and just knew there was a life beyond Mooseheart. The railroad track knew the way home, and someday I would find where I belonged.

Not only did we have to clean the hall, but we now had to work at a paying job. My first job was delivering the Chicago Tribune and Aurora Beacon News to the halls for twenty-five cents an hour. I would dilly dally while delivering the papers, sometimes stopping to sit under a tree and read the comics. The money I earned was deposited into my bank account. On Saturdays, I walked down to the bank to take out one cent to deposit in the church envelope.

I liked delivering papers as it was an antidote to hours of boredom. When I was eleven, my friend Jo Anne LaFrance and I were assigned to work at Muncie Hall, setting tables with Mrs. Hickman and babysitting. Working with her was refreshing; she was nice and didn't holler at us when something wasn't done perfectly.

After helping in the kitchen, we watched the younger children when they were playing outside at the playground across from Muncie Hall. One day, I was sitting on top of the freshly silver painted monkey bars when I heard a little boy named Bradley scream, "SUPERMAN" from the top of the red caboose that had Mooseheart painted in white letters. A Moose Club donated the railroad car to the playground for us to play on. I felt the same way; I was stuck on a lone railroad track, not going anywhere. The matrons told us the caboose was off limits, but Bradley had snuck away and climbed the steps to the roof when I wasn't watching.

After he had hit the ground, I slid down the leg of the monkey bars and screamed for help. When I saw him lying on the ground unconscious, with blood staining his reddish-blonde curls, I thought for sure he was dead. I ran across the street to tell the matron what happened. After the watchman had taken him to the hospital, the matron started screaming at me.

"You should have been watching him. You are good for nothing. Now I'm going to get in hot water for this."

When Bradley came back from the hospital with his head shaved and stitches running from the front to the back of his head I wished it would have been me who jumped from the caboose. If only I could get that picture out of mind. That night, I drifted off to sleep, feeling like I was a boy instead of a girl and my name was Peter. Just like Peter Pan, I could fly out the window to Neverland where lost boys lived.

The same year that I moved to East Legion Hall, my mother moved back to Loyalty Hall. After researching how meals were served at the Hershey Milton School in Pennsylvania, Mr. Ketz, the superintendent decided to build a centralized kitchen. Meals were no longer prepared in the halls but were delivered in stainless steel air void containers from the new centralized kitchen.

When I had kitchen duty in the hall, the stainless-steel metal truck drove up to the back door. The driver hauled the vacuum containers up the concrete steps and into the kitchen. When it was time to eat, we released the buckles to allow the steam to escape. The lingering odor of the seafood bisque we had the day before made me nauseous. The food smelled and tasted horribly. Much of it went into the garbage.

Thankfully, the cold fresh milk from the Mooseheart Dairy Farm was still delivered to the halls in large three-foot high stainless-steel milk cans. The cans were stored in a large stainless-steel cooler that dispensed the milk from a white rubber tube attached to the bottom of the can. Before each meal, large pitchers were filled with milk and set on the table.

For breakfast, we no longer had to eat pasty cream of wheat or cold oatmeal but were served cereal from nameless boxes. After finishing the cereal, we filled out a form to rank which cereal we liked best compared to the previous day. Every Saturday, one of us was assigned to walk to the commissary to pick up ice cream that was served with our Saturday evening supper.

In the summer, we were told to go to the high school for a popsicle treat. After standing in the sweltering sun for what seemed like hours, we were finally dispensed a popsicle in a plastic sleeve and were instructed to write down what flavor we liked best. They all tasted like plastic to me. We weren't only guinea pigs for food companies.

On a yearly basis, we went to the dentist's office to have dental molds for bone and teeth studies. Psychological tests were performed in an upstairs room of a vacant building. In the early years of Mooseheart, there was a stately building called "The Mooseheart Laboratory for Child Research" where psychological tests that measured levels of suggestibility by electric shock were administered. The tests were performed on children, against their will, by Martin L. Reymart and Harold Kohn. By the time I arrived at Mooseheart, the testing center was turned into a hall. Records were stored in the attic of the building and were eventually destroyed.

With the advent of the central kitchen, my mom and other mothers went from cooking in halls to working in the industrialized kitchen, peeling pounds and pounds of potatoes and scrubbing large stainless-steel pots and pans. The only warmth we felt at Mooseheart was mothers coming to the halls to cook, and now that was lost.

When I visited my mother back at Loyalty Hall, she was tired and sad. She met a new boyfriend named Art, who was hired to drive the stainless-steel truck that delivered food from the centralized kitchens around to the halls. Sometimes he would give me rides in the delivery truck. He bought beer for my brothers Jack and Bob.

Now my mom had three boyfriends, Fred, Arnie, and Art. Out of the three, I liked Art the best and wanted my mom to marry him so I would have a daddy. She said she couldn't marry him because he was already married.

New girls came to Mooseheart, but there was always a core group of us that had been there since we were three. Us 'lifers' showed the new girls the ropes, and in turn, they taught us a few things about the outside world. They introduced us to Ouija's boards and performed séances. We pierced our ears by freezing our lobes with ice and inserting a sterilized sewing needle and thread. I ended up with a large cyst behind my right ear that had to be removed surgically.

To curb the boredom of institution life, we stole cigarettes from the matrons and would sneak out the halls at night to meet boys. All of us dreamed and talked about how we were going to get out of Mooseheart someday.

Instead of the matrons punishing us for getting in trouble we now were sent to the girl's dean and received hours of punishment called "special." I didn't feel special when I sat for hours in a classroom while a lady sat and licked S&H green stamps into paper books. If we accumulated over one hundred hours of special, we were sent to a detention hall called the "farm." There were two kinds of farms at Mooseheart. One was a dairy farm, and the other were residences, one for boys and one for girls. There weren't any cows or horses, only isolation and hard work were in store for trouble makers.

I topped the one hundred hours when I refused to eat the food from the central kitchen. Because the girl's dean was on leave, the matron sent me to the boy's dean, Mr. Kershner. In a stern voice he asked, "Miss Van Zanten, I have a report in front of me that says you refused to eat your vegetables. Tell me why."

"I didn't eat the peas they sent because the food tastes like shit."

"Pack your clothes when you get back to the hall. You are going to the farm for two weeks."

The matrons at the farm were extremely strict and made us clean the hall that was already clean as a whistle. For lunch and supper, we had peanut butter sandwiches with no jelly and a boiled egg. Thankfully, there wasn't any food from the central kitchen. At school, the other kids weren't allowed to talk to us if we were on the farm. Spending two weeks on the farm was enough to deter me from complaining about the food. I learned to be more discreet and found ways to discard the food, such as folding it in a napkin and flushing it down the toilet when the matron left the room.

In the evenings, we looked forward to having Girl Scout meetings with Mrs. Graves, who was also the art teacher. She treated us to cookies and Kool-aid and taught us how to sew pillows by hand. A new girl, Lorraine Charbonneau moved to Mooseheart from Canada, and we became good friends. Lorraine was a strong-willed girl who didn't seem afraid of anything; not the matrons and not sneaking onto the boy's campus after the meetings. When the matron caught us, we were suspended from going to the Girl Scout meetings.

While we were outside playing during the daytime, Valerie and I couldn't get the railroad trestle nor freedom out of our minds. Dressed in our flowery orange and yellow bell bottoms with button down, sleeveless white blouses and black and white saddle shoes, we skipped the Saturday movie showing at the auditorium. Instead, we snuck down to the railroad tracks. Older kids told us that hobos slept under the trestle. I held the barbed wire fence for Valerie to crawl under. When she was on the other side, she did the same for me. We were headed to Aurora, Illinois only a few miles from Mooseheart.

When we didn't show up for supper at East Legion Hall, the matron alerted the watchman to track us down. A watchman nicknamed 'Weasel' hauled us back to the orphanage in the brown paneled station wagon. Running away wasn't the first episode of us getting into trouble.

Valerie seemed to have a hold on me since we were four years old and I wouldn't give her a plastic beach ball, she held my head under the water until I nearly drowned. Together, we were caught stealing soap from the dispensary and chewing gum from the Campanile. We made long chains from the wrappers and had contests to see who could make the longest one. One of the other kids was jealous because I had more wrappers and turned me in. Valerie and I spent quite a bit of time together on special and at the farm.

After the running away escapade and three days of isolation in our bedroom, Valerie didn't fare as well as I did. I had one living parent; she had no parents. She was a whole orphan and didn't have anyone to rely on. Valerie was sent to a girl's detention center in Indiana State. Mr. Ketz, the superintendent, strongly suggested that my mom take me out, or I would be sent to a detention center also. She convinced him that Valerie was the reason I got in so much trouble and that delayed my escape.

At school, I did well in all my classes except Spanish. The classroom had modules with headphones. Mrs. Kane listened in while we attempted to pronounce words in Spanish. I didn't roll my r's correctly, and when she insisted that I do it over and over, I became bored and frustrated and started saying swear words instead. When she heard me, I was removed from the Spanish class.

Mr. Baldwin, the music teacher, was a thin man with graying hair on the sides and a shiny bald head. He wore wire-rimmed glasses, a suit coat, dress pants, and tie. Music was a required course, and we all began on the piano. I did OK learning the basic notes, but since I didn't excel at the piano, Mr. Baldwin thought perhaps I would do better at the violin. I hated the screeching noise of the bow on the strings. It reminded me of squeaking chalk on a chalkboard and would send shivers up my spine. For practice, we were shut in a small room with glass windows, where a lady sitting at the desk could monitor us. It seemed like forever that we were locked in those little rooms. One day I brought in some glow in the dark silly putty and rubbed it on the bow to see what would happen. Lo and behold the violin didn't squeak anymore; in fact, it didn't make any noise.

When I arrived at band practice the next day, the secretary said, "Jeanette, have a seat next to my desk. Mr. Baldwin wants to see you."

My legs were freezing from the bitter Chicago wind because I refused to wear pants under my dress like I had to when I as was in elementary school.

Mr. Baldwin came out of his office, walked over to me and grabbed the hair in the back of my head. "Into my office young lady."

Without letting go of my hair, he pulled me into his office where there were large brass tubas, trombones, and trumpets. I began shivering as the freezing feeling that was in my legs traveled through my whole body. Mr. Baldwin picked up the violin bow and proceeded to tell me, "The strings on the bow are made of Palomino horse tail and are very expensive."

I knew what Palomino horses were because there was one at the horse farm where we rode horses. Charlie was a large Palomino that only the bigger girls, like Karen Maly, could ride. I was going to tell Mr. Baldwin that Charlie had a big tail that he swatted flies with, and I'm sure I could get some horse tail hair from him, but I was too frightened to speak. I dissociated and flew to the barn, jumped on Charlie's bareback and took off running through the pastures.

Mr. Baldwin was so mad; veins were popping out of his neck. "How in the world did you ruin a bow?" he asked.

"I don't remember."

He screamed, "You are lying!"

Then he made be bend over a chair and hit my bare legs with a long wooden paddle. "That's the board of education. Now get out and don't ever come back to this building again."

The only time I went back was when the 8th-grade girls tried out for the chorus. Mr. Baldwin didn't let me try out, which was probably a good thing because I couldn't carry a note. He pointed his finger toward the door and said, "Leave."

I left.

Since I was still required to take music, I was turned over to Mr. Schwartz, a short, stout, jolly fellow who always had a smile on his face. He taught me how to play the clarinet and at the end of a lesson he encouragingly said, "You're coming along nicely. Would you like to join the marching band?" I was fitted with a band uniform that was a little too big because they didn't have one my size. I joined the other students marching in parades and at football games.

Although my first attempt at freedom by trying to run away with Valerie didn't succeed, I felt like a fledgling bird getting it's wings. I pondered on the birds that flew free in the sky and wondered where they went after they left the confines of the Mooseheart.

Again, a poem by Victor Hugo that I found later in my life reminded me of what I went through during this time.

Be like a bird,

That, pausing in her flight

Awhile on boughs too slight,

Feels them give a way beneath her and yet sings

Knowing she has wings.

Chapter Six

———•————————•———

When it came time for graduation from elementary school, Mrs. Gulley insisted I have a new dress for the occasion. Since my mom wasn't good at shopping, Mrs. Gulley offered to take me shopping. I had never been in a store before and was overwhelmed with all the smells, lights, and shiny floors. Mrs. Gulley took my hand and walked me to the girl's clothing section and said, "Honey, you pick out any dress you would like to wear for your graduation."

I was unable to move. Words wouldn't come out of my mouth. I had never picked out a dress or anything to wear in my whole life. Mrs. Gulley sensed my anxiety. When I couldn't make a decision, she held up two dresses and asked which one I liked the best. I pointed to the light blue and white plaid jumper with a lacy white top underneath.

I looked around to find my mom, but she was gone. Mrs. Gulley then picked out a pair of nylons, a garter belt, and my very first bra. We found my mom wandering around the store, and when we went to pay for the clothes, my mom told Mrs. Gulley, she didn't have any money. Mrs. Gulley said, "Oh that's Ok, I'll just put it on my card."

When I got back to the hall and tried on my new clothes, they all fit perfectly except for the nylons that slid down my skinny legs. Before the graduation ceremony, we went to the beauty shop, where the high school girls cut and curled our hair and sprayed it with a lot of hair spray.

Mrs. Gulley and her nine-year-old granddaughter attended the graduation with my mom. Mrs. Gulley was smiling ear to ear, during the ceremony and afterward gave me one of her big warm hugs. "Honey, I am so proud that you graduated to the middle school. You are a smart young lady, and you will do well in your classes next year." I wondered how she knew how to say such meaningful things to me compared to my mom.

After graduation, I moved to Mississippi Hall which bordered the high school girl's campus. Now that I was getting older, I had more freedom on the campus and was allowed to go out without a permit to ride my bike to the girl's gym where I jumped on the trampoline and shot archery.

I also took swim lessons at the newly built indoor pool. My gym teacher, Miss Goldstein, who we nicknamed "Goldie" always had a smile on her face when we arrived for swim lessons. She cheered us on as we swam laps from one end of the pool to the other so that we could qualify to go into the deep end of the pool. When we attained that goal, she taught us how to dive off of the diving board and challenged us to do back dives and flips. Our first bathing suits were red cotton, one-piece suits that were heavy, especially when wet. Goldie got permission for us to wear two-piece bathing suits called bikinis.

My first attempt at a back dive wasn't a success. One, two, three… I counted the steps up to the diving board. Feeling confident, I walked the gritty plank three paces and took a deep breath so I could calculate the next three steps to the edge of the board that hung over the pool of sparkling water.

I turned backwards and balanced on my tiptoes, spreading my arms like a fledging ready to leave its nest. To gauge the spring of the board, and gain some momentum, I bounced up and down a couple of times. Front dives and flips were familiar to me, but I had never attempted a back dive before. I sprung into the air and quickly turned my hands and head downwards to form a dive. CRACK! My head hit the board, and my body smacked onto the water that felt like a piece of concrete!

Goldie's whistle echoed off the walls. When I opened my eyes, a large white operating light blinded me and a man wearing a white coat, black hair and black plastic framed glasses was stitching the top of my head closed.

When I wasn't allowed in the pool after the diving accident, I became bored and talked my friend Mimi Maly into riding our bikes out to see my brother Jack, who worked at the dairy farm. The smell of the hay and fodder in the barn reminded both my brother and me of the farm we had lived on before we went to Mooseheart.

Mimi and I told the matrons we would be going to ride horses, but first, we headed to the heifer barn to see Jack. I could count on him to say, "Hey Jeanette, help me scoop up this cow shit," as he handed me a shovel. I grabbed a shovel propped in the corner and handed it to Mimi. While the black and white Holstein cows chewed their cud, and swatted us with their tails, we both shoveled piles of manure from the trenches, into a wheelbarrow that Jack hauled away.

Cleaning the barn was better than the chores we had to do at the halls. The barn work felt purposeful and wasn't boring. Plus, we didn't have matrons breathing down our necks.

After all the manure was cleaned up, Jack gave us both a hot soapy bucket of water and showed us how to clean the cow's tails. While we were busy working, a man's deep voice startled me. I thought for sure we were in trouble until he said: "Hey Van Zanten, I'll have to start calling you Tom Sawyer, getting these girls to do your work for you."

Jack snickered, "Yeah, you don't even have to put them on the payroll." I looked up to see a tall man with sandy-colored hair, a shade lighter than his tanned skin, with his hands in the pockets of his blue jean bib overalls. Jack introduced the two of us girls to Mr. Klussendorf.

"Hey, Mr. Klussendorf, you have the same name as my teacher Mrs. Klussendorf," I said.

"That's my wife. You can call me Dell. This isn't a school; it's a barn."

He turned to Jack and said, "Have them brush these calves that we'll be taking to the fair."

When Jack beckoned me to go into a stall with the calves, I backed away. I felt more at ease when he showed me how to put my hand in their mouth so they would suck my fingers. "See, they don't have teeth to bite you like a horse does." I did just what he told me and put my hand in the warm, wet calf's mouth to feel the tongue that felt like sandpaper. Jack put a halter on the calf and taught us how to lead the calves around the stall.

When Dell saw how good we were doing with the cows he told Jack, "I'll have to get permission to take these girls to the fair."

I said, "Now that would be a miracle. Girls aren't even supposed to be at the dairy barn, and you are going to take us to a fair? I have never been to a fair in my whole life. Only boys get to do that."

Dell winked at me and said, "I'll see what I can do."

When the other girls at the hall heard Mimi and I talking about playing in the hayloft, petting kittens and brushing the cows, they all asked if they could go with us. We picked out a couple of girls that weren't too prissy and afraid of getting dirty. Dell always had a smile on his face when he saw us skipping towards the barn.

After our chores, he took us into the milk house and gave us big glasses of chocolate milk. I asked him "Does chocolate milk come from brown cows?"

"Who told you that?" he asked.

"My brother Bill. He used to work here before he graduated."

"That Van Zanten boy was full of it. Don't you believe a word he told you." I was glad that he felt the same way about Bill that I did.

After Dell saw how hard girls can work, he told me and two of my friends he wanted to talk to us. We thought for sure we were in trouble.

Maybe he found out we snuck up into the hayloft to pet the kittens and jump in the hale bales.

Instead he said, "I got special permission for you girls to show the calves at the fair this year. If you get one of your moms to go with us, you can go." I looked around at the other two girls that didn't have moms and knew he was talking about my mom. I raised my hand and said, "I'll ask my mom."

"Remember, you aren't in school here. The show will be in a month, so get back to me after talking to your mom. She likes to come out here and see Jack, so I'm sure it won't be a problem."

The next time I saw my mom, I asked her if she would go with us to the fair to show the calves. She agreed! I would learn many years later, that my mom was raised on a dairy farm and knew all about cows, barns and fairs.

In the coming weeks, we spent every free minute up at the barn. Dell stressed to us the importance of the fair, as Mooseheart had one of the top dairy herds in the state, with cows milking up to 80-100 pounds of milk a day. He brought us into the milking room to show us a wall of large blue ribbons that were won at the Illinois State Fair in Springfield, Illinois.

The day before the fair we washed the calves and cleaned out their stalls. Jack showed us how to put a halter on the animals and lead them with a rope. After getting our toes stepped on a few times, we learned how to keep an eye on our feet.

The next day, my mom drove us to the local Black and White Holstein Show at the Kane County fairgrounds in St. Charles. We brushed the black and white calves, making sure they were clean. Jack teased us and asked if we wanted to put a ribbon on their tails.

After walking the calves around the ring, we were surprised to win three blue ribbons at the fair for showing the calves. In the milking room, Dell hung up a Polaroid picture of the first girls from Mooseheart at a dairy show We were all so proud of ourselves and thankful to Dell for believing in us.

In the winter, the days were long and boring without anything to do after school. Peggy Davis and I decided to steal some of the matron's cigarettes and take them up into the attic of the hall to smoke. There weren't steps to the crawl space, so we got on the shoulders of one of the taller girls and hiked ourselves up into the ceiling. When we got into the attic, there were only boards and fluffy gray stuff. Not knowing that we would fall through the ceiling if we didn't stay on the boards, we took one step and fell right through the ceiling onto the floor with gray stuff falling like snow.

We knew we were in trouble when the matron came running up the steps screaming, "What is going on up here?"

The other girls scrambled to hide the cigarettes, along with the instant coffee we had swiped from the kitchen. Peggy and I sat in the middle of a pile of cracked ceiling and gray stuff and didn't have an excuse, so we told her that one of the other girls dared us to go up into the attic.

The matron pushed her glasses up on her nose, pulled her cotton dress down to straighten out the wrinkles and put her hands on her hips. "Would you go jump off a bridge if someone told you to?" I wanted to tell her "*probably*" but shook my head no.

"Both of you are headed to the dean's office. No, instead I'm calling her to see this mess for herself."

Within an hour, the girl's dean pulled up in front of the house and clomped up the steps with her oxford shoes. She had white hair that was cropped and looked like a man's haircut.

"What is going on here?" she asked in a stern, but not a screaming voice like the matron. The matron didn't give us a chance to speak and told her everything that had happened.

The dean said, "You girls get busy and clean this mess up." We thought for sure we were headed for the farm, but instead, she continued,

"And you will be working to pay for the repairs. What you don't pay for, your parent's will pay for."

"I don't have a parent." Peggy answered.

"Well you have a guardian, and they will pay for it," answered the dean.

There wasn't much work for us that winter, but when summer arrived, Peggy and I were assigned to the high school every day to scrub down desks and chairs during summer break.

My brother Bob would be graduating in June and was working on getting his driver's license. While visiting my mom on a boring Sunday afternoon, he wanted to drive the car, but she told him he wasn't allowed to drive the car on the campus. Since she didn't have a permit to take us off campus, she took us for a ride around the lake.

Bob got in the front passenger seat of the mint green Rambler. I sat on the left side behind my mom and Warren sat on the right side behind Bob. Jack was on the farm so he wasn't with us. We puttered around the lake, passing the spill dam until we came to a bend where there was a Y. Another car was behind us and took the opposite road. As both cars were approaching the intersection, my brother Bob barked orders at my mom. He shouted, "Step on the gas to beat that other car to the intersection."

She listened and stepped on the gas, which sent the car flying straight into a tree. I flew into the back of the front seat banging my head on something hard and sharp. I looked up to see shattered glass and heard the car horn blaring. My mom was slumped over the steering wheel. The other car stopped to see if we were ok. Bob got out of the car and went over to talk to them. They drove off to get help.

It seemed like forever as we waited for someone to arrive. The watchman piled us all into his car and took us to the hospital where the doctor stitched up a three-inch cut on my forehead. Bob lost some teeth and Warren was pretty shaken up. We all had to stay overnight at the hospital for observation.

My brother Jack was serving detention for some misdemeanor by cleaning at the hospital and came into the girl's room to see how I was. I asked him if our mom was killed and he got permission to walk me down to her room to see her.

When she saw my head wrapped in white gauze, I saw a tear in her eye. Her right hand was wrapped in gauze and her face was bruised. We didn't go for rides with my mom again, until she was able to get a new car. She bought an army green Rambler. As much as I liked to get out of Mooseheart, I was hesitant to ride with her after the accident and found excuses to spend time with my friends.

On July 20th 1969,the first man landed on the moon, and we watched it on television at the halls. We all sat cross-legged on the floor, and listened to the voice of Neil Armstrong crackle, "That's one small step for a man, one giant leap for mankind." I wondered how someone could get off this planet when I couldn't figure out how to get out of Mooseheart.

That summer I was called to the Campanile, which was the visitor's center located at the entrance of Mooseheart. The matron told me to wear nice clothes as there was someone special who wanted to see me.

When I arrived at the Campanile, a woman wearing a red dress, shiny black high heels and hair piled on top of her head, like Mrs. Gulley wore her hair, walked over to me and introduced herself as Mrs. Bassett. A man with gray hair was standing beside her wearing a suit and tie and an overcoat. Mrs. Davidge, who was in charge of the Campanile, told me that Mr. and Mrs. Bassett were from Pennsylvania and would be Sunshine Parents. I thought that only kids without any parents were matched with Sunshine Parents, who visited, wrote letters and bought gifts for their "adopted" orphan.

I was instructed to give the couple a tour of Mooseheart. I got in the back of the big car that had a roomy back seat and directed them around the campus to see the school, the dairy farm, the lake and the hall in which I lived. Mr. Bassett told me that they picked my name from the list of

Mooseheart kids because my middle name, Elizabeth, was the same as his wife's first name and I was from Pennsylvania. He told me his wife was very sad because she couldn't have children.

Mrs. Bassett didn't talk very much but gave me a stuffed dog that had a radio inside of it. After the couple dropped me off at my hall, I wrote them a thank you letter for the dog, and she sent me a picture of her and her husband. She asked me what I wanted for Christmas, and I told her an electric hair dryer, which she sent to me. I tried to write nice letters, hoping the couple would adopt me, but when I started asking them to help me get out of Mooseheart, they ended contact.

The next hall I was assigned to was Massachusetts Hall. It was a large two-story building where we had rooms instead of dormitories. My room-mate was Lorraine Charbonneau. At night, we would listen to WKBI on the radio and stay up late talking and laughing. Because the hall was spacious and the rooms were separated, the matrons couldn't hear us, so we didn't have to worry about having to scrub the floors on our hands and knees.

After the matron hollered at us to turn the lights out, Lorraine gave her the middle finger. I asked her what that meant, and she said in French it meant "stick it." Lorraine told me that her mom had a boyfriend and was going to take her out of Mooseheart as soon as she could. I asked her if she would take me with her. She promised me she would talk to her mom.

Our stay at Massachusetts Hall was short because on Christmas Day there was a fire at the hall. I was visiting my mom at Loyalty Hall and had just finished opening a Christmas present when we heard the fire sirens. My brothers and I ran out of Loyalty Hall to see smoke billowing out of a bedroom window located next to my room at Massachusetts Hall. I ran up to the hall and stood outside in the cold as I watched fire trucks shoot water to put out the flames.

As smoke poured out of the two-story concrete structure with red tile roofing, I wished the whole place would burn down. We had attempted to start fires while playing outside on more than one occasion, ending up with more punishment than any child deserved.

When the coast was clear, and people were going in and out of the building, I ran up to my bedroom to see if my clothes were still there. I was happy the fire was contained to the room next to mine, but the hall reeked of smoke, and the floors and walls were water damaged.

We later found out the cause of the fire. Tammy Ruple had lit a candle next to a curtain that caught on fire. The hall was evacuated, and the ten of us girls had to move into the vacant New Jersey boy's hall. We thought we were cool living on the boy's campus.

What wasn't cool was the new matron who was instructed to keep a strict watch on us-and that she did. I spent many hours in a dank, dark basement with a light bulb above my head, sitting at an old wooden school desk, copying scriptures from the Bible. My offense was wearing my street shoes, instead of my slippers in the house.

While we were in New Jersey Hall, Lorraine was fitted with a back brace for scoliosis. At night time, I helped her get the back brace off, and in the morning I helped put it on because she didn't want to ask the matron for help.

True to what Lorraine told me, her mom took her out of Mooseheart. When she left, we hugged, and with tears streaming down her cheeks, she said, "I asked my mom if you could come with us, but she said you couldn't. I'll miss you, Van. You are the best friend I ever had." Lorraine came back to visit a few times and tracked me down on campus. She had back surgery and was in a full cast, but told me how happy she was not being at Mooseheart.

When school started in the fall, I felt lost without Lorraine but, as usual enjoyed my classes. Now that we were in seventh grade the girls took home economic class, and the boys took shop class. The first semester, Miss Mae Miller taught us how to cut out patterns and use a sewing machine. My first sewing project was a poncho made from a striped lavender fabric.

The second semester we had a cooking class where we learned to read and follow recipes. Miss Miller told me I had nice handwriting and had me print recipes on large pieces of cardboard for the class to follow.

Miss Miller also gave me a reference for a summer job to work at the cafeteria in the Campanile where I served lunches to the people who worked at the Supreme Court Lodge. After the employees were finished eating, the ladies who worked in the cafeteria let us have leftover cottage cheese salads with peaches. I wondered why the employees didn't have to eat the food from the Central Kitchen. I also worked long hours at the Supreme Lodge stuffing envelopes with propaganda about Mooseheart.

After I was finished working at the Moose Lodge, I walked through the high school girl's campus where the teenage girls sunbathed in their bikinis; their legs and arms glistening from Johnson Baby Oil mixed with Iodine.

I found an isolated place behind some trees where I could lay on the lawn and daydream. Instead of a bikini, I was wearing a sleeveless plaid button-down blouse, blue jean cut-offs rolled up, just above my knees, a white canvas pair of cheap tennis shoes with white ankle socks that slid down underneath my heels. With my hands clasped behind my head of brunette, fine hair that I was trying to grow out from a short, Twiggy style pixie, I looked up at the sky with billowing white clouds and found myself talking to God.

With tears streaming down my cheeks I cried out, "Why can't I be free like the clouds? I don't like the fences around me. I don't like all the rules. I don't like feeling lonely, abandoned and lost. Where the hell are you?" This was my first real prayer to God.

Just a month earlier Kathy Brasch, another friend of mine-we'd known each other since we were three years-cross pinky bet that we wouldn't cry when our brothers, Rick and Jack, graduated from the high school at Mooseheart. I just knew I would win the bet. I didn't cry any tears in 1969 when my brother Bob graduated and left. I didn't cry in 1966 when my two brothers, Paul and Bill graduated and left. And I didn't shed a tear in 1963 when my sister Ginny graduated and left.

Our brothers graduated a month after we watched the Kent State Massacre on television. I was still feeling numb from watching the four college students being gunned down and nine others wounded while they were protesting the Vietnam war.

I felt as if I could hear the rumbling of protestors at Kent State University, only two states away in Ohio. As the 1970 senior class of Mooseheart, dressed in maroon caps and gowns, marched into the field house, I silently sobbed to the marching ballad of Pomp and Circumstance. I had lost the bet with Kathy

Out of my five brothers, Jack was the one I got along with best. Although he did his share of teasing, he did more than make fun of me. He had social skills that my other brothers didn't. He asked how my classes were and took an interest in my friends.

One of my friends, Chris Turcotte, a thin blonde girl from Canada who had twelve brothers and sisters, came to Mooseheart when she was ten. The two of us walked to the canteen together to buy candy and visit our brothers on Saturday afternoons. I attended Jack's track meets at the Mooseheart football field, where I could always spot his tall, thin frame and hair the same shade of brown as mine.

After graduation, Jack received his draft number. It was five. He decided to enlist in the Army, hoping he would be stationed in Germany or Italy. After basic training he was assigned to Vietnam. Everyone at Mooseheart knew about the Vietnam war because Tim Gilson, a Mooseheart grad, was killed in 1969. Tim's sister Ruby was a year older than me. I'll never forget the day she received the news that her brother was killed. Her wailing and sobbing shook the concrete walls of Massachusetts Hall.

Afterward, all of the students on campus gathered in the auditorium to see Mrs. Gilson receive the Purple Heart Medal in honor of her son.

My mother was best friends with Tim Gilson's mom, and they both cried when Jack was drafted into the army. When I visited my mom at her apartment at Loyalty Hall, she would be lying on her bed listening to *The Green Beret Ballad*. The lights were off and the white shade pulled down. I sat on the couch in the dark room and watched the vinyl record turn around and around on a portable turntable. Jack's absence left my brother Warren, who would graduate in 1973, and me, the caboose of the family alone with our grieving mother at Mooseheart.

I came to the conclusion that there were only three ways to get out of Mooseheart. Adoption wasn't an option because the institution needed our social security money to keep operating. Also, the majority of kids had one parent living, which made us half orphans, making it difficult to get adopted. The first way to get out of Mooseheart was to graduate from high school. The second way was to get kicked out for breaking the rules, and the third way was to get an older sibling to help us get out. I opted for a combination of the latter two.

Getting into trouble worked for my friend Tammy Ruple, labeled an incorrigible girl by the matrons. Tammy and I came to Mooseheart in 1961 when we were both three years old. Her home state was Michigan. It was only a few months after the fire incident that Tammy's older sister Marcia provided a home for her in Michigan.

For me, my sister Ginny was out of the question. She married her boyfriend from Mooseheart and was in Connecticut with little children. After our father had died, Ginny liked the idea that we were going to Mooseheart and she liked it there. She made friends and didn't have to put up with living with siblings anymore. Bill was out of the question also. He was working on a dairy farm in Pennsylvania. He teased me incessantly, calling me names, pulling my hair and told me stories that weren't true. I was so angry when I was old enough to figure out the lie he had told me about brown cows giving chocolate milk. Both Ginny and Bill seemed to like Mooseheart and weren't about to help me out. I didn't know where my brother Bob was living.

My oldest brother Paul hated Mooseheart as much as I did. I knew if anyone could get me out of there it would be him. He and his girlfriend Dottie had recently moved to St. Marys, Pennsylvania. Paul landed a job at a powdered metal factory, and Dottie was hired as an RN at the hospital. I started writing letters to the two of them telling them about all of my troubles and how much I wanted to get out of Mooseheart. At first, they didn't receive the letters because the mail at Mooseheart was censored. So instead, I started giving my mom the letters to send when she went to St. Charles, Illinois to visit her boyfriend, Arnie.

My mom took a vacation to see Paul and Dottie in St. Marys and lent them a five-thousand dollar down payment she had saved from her social security and meager earnings at Mooseheart for a house on 123 Parade Street. It was a duplex, and I would be living upstairs with her, my brother Warren and my brother Bob.

My prayers were answered. The last ten years of my life were spent as an insider. Now I would be living on the outside. No more matrons, no more chain linked fences, no more whistles blowing to wake me up in the morning, no more permits to go from one place to another, no more detention for disobeying. After ten years of incarceration, I would begin my teen-age years as free as a bird. I was ready to fly, but my wings weren't very strong, nor did I have a nest to return to when I would fall.

PART TWO

Chapter Seven

On a sunny day in July wearing blue jean cut off shorts, rolled up shorter than allowed by the girl's dean and a green cotton tank top with my bra straps showing, I packed my clothes in a large cardboard moving box and tucked school photographs of my friends Veda York, Peggy Davis, Mimi Maly, her big sister Karen Maly, Christine Turcotte, Lorraine Charbonneau and Tammy Ruple into an envelope.

After all my belongings were packed, my friend Joanne LaFrance gave me her school picture and a big hug. I slid the black and white photograph into the back pocket of my blue jean shorts. I hugged her and told her I that would write to her.

I sat on the concrete porch of the last hall I would be staying in, anxiously waiting for my brother Paul, who was now twenty-one years old, to pick me up in a candy apple red Ford pick-up truck that belonged to my brother Bill. When the truck pulled up in front of the hall, I lugged the cardboard box containing all my earthly belongings, down the fifteen concrete steps. Paul lifted it up into the back of the truck for me. Without permission from the matron-they wouldn't be bossing me around anymore-I got in the front seat of the truck.

After picking up my brother Warren on the boy's campus, Paul drove down to Loyalty Hall where my mother had a small apartment. Even though she knew this was moving day, she had nothing packed. Paul tossed her small collection of plastic dishes, a White sewing machine, a Kirby sweeper my father had bought her, a framed aerial photograph of the farmhouse that the government had seized and a black trunk filled with salvaged bedding from our homestead before we were exiled to Mooseheart, into the back of truck.

There wasn't room for my small, white musical rocking chair. It was tossed into the garbage; I felt as if my heart was thrown away. The chair was the only relic I had from my father. He gave it to me for my third birthday on August 21, 1960, two months before he died.

When we exited the gates of Mooseheart, Paul didn't stop at the guard house to show the guards the permit needed to leave the grounds. As we headed toward Aurora, I sat by the passenger door of the pick-up truck and kept looking in the oblong rear view mirror to make sure that no guards from the orphanage were following us. We drove to Naperville, Illinois to stay overnight at Mr. and Mrs. Gulley's house before we would make our trek to Pennsylvania.

Alma, Mrs. Gulley and her husband Charlie, Mr. Gulley were my brother Jack's house parents when he was in Maryland-Delaware Hall at Mooseheart. In the orphanage, boys had houseparents, consisting of a couple who were married, giving them a male influence in their lives. The girls only had matrons. I guess we didn't need father figures, but boys needed a mother figure.

The Gulley's were at Mooseheart for five years, long enough for my brother Warren to get assigned to their hall. They left Mooseheart, because the administration put in the centralized kitchen and food was no longer prepared in the halls. Mr. Gulley had diabetes and didn't fare well on the institutionalized food. For a while, the couple bought food for the boys in their hall, but feeding a dozen growing boys soon became unaffordable for them.

After Mr. and Mrs. Gulley left Mooseheart, my mom obtained a special permit to visit them on a farm they rented within a few miles of Mooseheart. They had horses and a pond where their granddaughter Shelley, who was a few years younger than me, would throw rocks.

Whenever I would ask Mrs. Gulley for permission to do something, she said, "Honey you don't need to tell me everything. You just go on and have fun while you are here."

Her son, big Tommy Jo was a truck driver and needed his name embroidered on the uniform shirts he wore. My mom told Mrs. Gulley that I liked to embroidery, so she paid me real money to sew his name on the shirts. Before I returned to Mooseheart at night, Mrs. Gulley took me to the store to spend the money on whatever I wanted. I bought more thread and a pillow case to embroider.

When we pulled in their driveway with the red pick-up truck loaded with all our belongings, Mrs. Gulley said we looked like the Beverly Hillbillies; and all we needed was a rocking chair on top of the truck. I started to feel sad about the rocking chair Paul threw out, until Shelley came skipping out of the house and grabbed my hand leading me to feed the horses.

My first night out of Mooseheart, Shelley and I slept together in the attic. Mrs. Gulley had made up a bed for us in a little cove with a window. I told Shelley I wanted to sleep by the window. She wore pajamas and I slept in my clothes. I had read stories in my history classes about the Underground Railroad where slaves had to get up in the middle of the night to move from one place to the other so they could escape quickly. I didn't sleep much that night as I watched out the window for the Mooseheart guard to pull up in the driveway to take me back. Thankfully that didn't happen.

The next morning, I woke up to the smell of bacon cooking. When I came down, Granny had her apron on, and was cooking breakfast for over ten people. I helped her butter the toast just as I was trained to do at Mooseheart.

After breakfast, it was time to leave. I wished I could have stayed right there with Mr. and Mrs. Gulley and Granny. When she hugged me goodbye, I didn't want to let her go. "We'll see you again honey. Write me letters and let me know how you all are doing."

She gave me a little heart shaped jewelry box, lined with red velvet. The top had a blue background and a white ship embossed on it. She told me it reminded her of my Dutch heritage. I don't remember if I ever wrote her a letter, but I thought of her each time I looked at the jewelry box that I carried with me for many years.

My brother Bob drove my mother's army green 1968 Rambler the 700 miles it would take to get to Pennsylvania from Illinois. My mom tried to get me to ride in the car, but I didn't want to be with her or my brother. Neither did Warren.

For the first hour, I didn't take my eyes off the rear-view mirror. After crossing the Indiana state border and not seeing the watchman's familiar brown paneled paddy wagon, I knew I was free.

Riding seventy miles an hour with the truck window rolled down and the air blowing in my face, I sang to myself "Born free, as free as the winds blow, as free as the grass grows, born free to follow my heart." I didn't think ahead of what it would be like to live in a house without rules and a mother who was mentally ill and an alcoholic.

The radio in the truck was set at 94.7. Wolfman Jack's raspy voice and the familiar voices of the Carpenter's singing *Close To You* from the WLS station began to fade at the same time as did the memories of all my friends. Paul shoved an eight-track tape into the tape deck dangling from the console of the truck. Johnny Cash's deep voice began singing *The Folsom Prison Blues*.

As he lit up a Kent cigarette, Paul said, "Wait until you hear the next song, Brat. It's about a Camp Cornplanter in Pennsylvania where they take retarded kids like you."

I tried to ignore him and stared at my reflection in the rearview mirror. A lost, lonely girl with greasy brown hair, cut in a short bob with bangs stared back at me.

Who was I? Was I Van, the tom-boy who had to live up to her brother's mischievous ways? Was I Twiggy, the little girl who tried to starve herself to death? Was I Brat, the little girl who was sexually abused? Was I Jeanette, the little girl who liked to write and printed perfectly after the first-grade teacher put clothespins on her ears and made her stand out in the hallway for not making her K's correctly? Was I Caroline, the little girl who the matron screamed: "I'll shake you like a dog shakes a rabbit" while she shook her head back and forth? Was I Elizabeth, the little girl who loved nature and animals and lived on a farm a long time ago?

Not having an answer, I floated up to the dark clouds ahead that forecasted rain and heavy thundershowers and thought about who I could be that was someone new. It had to be someone that wouldn't remember any of the past. Liz-that's who I would be now. Liz would be tough and wouldn't take shit from anyone, not even her brother's calling her retarded.

After three hours of sitting in the truck, I was glad to stop at a rest stop to use the bathroom. My bladder felt like a water balloon that was ready to bust. I could feel the stiff sanitary napkin becoming wet between my legs. When I got to the toilet and pulled down my sweaty, blue jean cut off shorts, I quickly untangled the sanitary napkin from the clasps that held the ends.

While sitting on the toilet, I pulled out the photo Joanne LaFrance had given me before I left. I turned it over to read what she wrote on the back.

Dear Van,

It was a blast working with you at Muncie Hall. You are a good friend. We had a lot of fun times. I will miss you.

Your friend, Joanne

Just as I was finishing up in the bathroom, I heard Paul outside the door hollering "Brat, what the hell are you doing in there?" I hadn't thought ahead to pack extra sanitary napkins. I tossed the soiled pad into the toilet and rolled toilet paper around my hand until it was an inch thick. I tucked the wad of toilet paper in my underwear, pulled up my pants and the zipper as I hurried out to the truck.

Paul said I would have to eat in the truck because he had to get back in time to go to work in the morning. I grabbed a can of Crush soda and a ham sandwich out of the green, metal cooler and hopped back into the truck.

I unwrapped the soggy sandwich and ate it in a few bites. At the next rest stop, Warren said he wanted to sit by the window. I didn't mind because I was tired of looking at the lost girl in the mirror. The Johnny Cash eight-track tape was playing for the twentieth time, and my head was dizzy from the smell of the cigarette smoke, so I began to sing a Peter, Paul, and Mary tune to myself.

"Lord I'm one, Lord I'm two, Lord I'm three, Lord, I'm four, Lord I'm five hundred miles from my home. Five hundred miles, five hundred miles, five hundred miles, Lord I'm five hundred miles from my home. Not a shirt on my back, not a penny to my name. Lord, I can't go home this away."
The flat landscape of Indiana and Ohio finally turned into beautifully sculpted mountains that felt like home. I itched to take off my shoes and run through the cold creeks just as I did before my father died. By evening, my tummy was growling, and I wondered where we would get food to

eat without the central kitchen delivering meals in air void containers to the halls.

"Hey Brat, do you want some pizza?" Paul asked.

"I don't know." If I answered yes, he might tell me to make it myself.

Paul put the left turn signal on and turned into a plaza and parked the truck in front of the bright orange neon light in large letters that read GARY'S PIZZA. He got out of the truck and said: "I'll be right back."

After about a half an hour of me sitting in the truck, he came back with a large rectangular box that was steaming hot and told me to hold it. The bottoms of my legs were sticky from sitting in the truck so long. The heat from the pizza box was burning the top of my legs. I bit my bottom lip and slid my hands under the box to shield my legs from the heat. The aroma of the pizza made my tummy growl even louder.

"Give me a piece of that pizza, Brat."

"I can't, I'm holding the box."

"You're a dipshit."

When we got into St. Marys, Paul took a right and then another right and parked the truck across from a large building that said *United States Post Office*. He ejected the eight-track tape and left the truck running, opened the door and got out of the truck. Holding the door open, he said, "Hey Warren, you want to go into Blacky's with me to get some beer?" Warren jumped out of the truck, and Paul slammed the door, leaving me in the truck by myself.

I was used to sitting and doing nothing for hours for punishment at Mooseheart. When we didn't follow the rules, talked back, or were late for meals we received hours of "special" that required us to sit in a school room with a fat, plump, short woman named Mrs. Springer who looked like Aunt Bea from the Andy Griffith show, although she wasn't near as nice. She sat at a desk licking green stamps while we weren't allowed to talk, read or draw. With that being next to impossible, she would occasionally look around the room and add hours to whoever wasn't compliant. We just had to sit and do nothing.

After I had accumulated up to one-hundred hours of sitting, I would gaze out the windows of the schoolroom and watch the other children play outdoors and was confused as to why I was special and they weren't. Years later I would learn that sitting and observing thoughts was a coveted meditation practice

As I balanced the pizza on my lap, I reached over and turned the black ridged radio knob until I heard the familiar Mr. Bo Jangles song. I stared at the neon orange marker at 93.9, the WKBI radio station and waited until Paul came out of the bar carrying a six pack of Straub beer. When Warren and him returned to the truck, the smell of beer on his breath made me want to vomit. I held my nostrils together with my forefinger and thumb to block the smell.

Thankfully we were only a few minutes away from our new house in St. Mary's. When we arrived at the house, Paul started beeping the horn and then pulled into a narrow driveway beside the two-story house. He stopped the truck and grabbed the pizza box. "C'mon Brat, let's say hi to Dottie." I peeled my thigh off the seat and climbed out of the truck. The cool night air of Pennsylvania was refreshing.

Bob and my mom pulled into the driveway behind us. Bob got out of the car and lit up a Camel cigarette with his silver Zippo lighter, clicked it shut and slipped it into his jean pocket. "I'm going back down to Blacky's. See you guys later."

I followed Paul into the large, two-story, white house through the double glass French doors with white nylon curtains. A little brown short haired mutt named Kippy, but should have been named Yippy, barked and barked. I was still a little skittish after getting attacked by a German Shepherd Paul and Dottie had while they were living in Rockford, Illinois. I was running around the yard playing, and the dog started running after me and grabbed my flowery bell bottom pants with it's sharp teeth and strong jaw. The bite tore my pants and broke the skin on my ankle.

Dottie came out of the kitchen and into the living room still dressed in her white nurse uniform, white nylon stockings and her hair wrapped in a bun. She had just finished working the 3-11 shift at the Andrew Kaul Memorial Hospital.

"Hi, Brat. What took you guys so long? I thought you would be here by now." She took the pizza from me and put it on the table in the kitchen. Everyone grabbed a paper plate and filled their plates with pizza. I was thirsty, but there was only Straub beer from the local brewery, in the fridge to drink. Paul handed me a green bottle of beer and told me to take a drink, so I did but almost threw up on the taste. When no one was looking, I went back outside and got a warm pop from the cooler in the truck.

On the way out to the truck, I noticed a bathroom. After I was done eating three pieces of pizza and drinking the warm pop, I went into to use the restroom. The toilet paper wad that served as a sanitary napkin was soaked. I looked in the cupboard under the sink and was relieved to find a fresh package of Modest pads. The pads were softer than the cardboard-issued ones at Mooseheart. I changed the pad and stuck a few extra in the waistband of my shorts.

On my second night out of Mooseheart I slept in the bunk of a truck camper parked next to the house. As the sun began to rise, I laid on the canvas covered foam mattress and waited for a whistle to blow so that I could get out of bed. Instead, I was wakened by the sound of a neighbor's lawn mower and the smell of fresh cut grass. I scrambled out of the camper excited to see what a free world looked like.

Two tall maple trees shaded the house. In my barefeet, I walked up the street to see a real neighborhood. No one was outside. All the houses were pretty, but not too fancy. At the end of the street was a little convenience store named Vito's Hoagies. I turned around and skipped back to the new house singing "Born free, free as the wind blows. Born free to follow my heart."

When I returned to the house, I went into the downstairs kitchen of the duplex to find Paul and Dottie sitting at the kitchen table smoking Kent cigarettes and drinking coffee.

"Hey Brat, how did you sleep?" Paul asked.

"OK," I answered. "Where's my room?" Paul had promised me that I would have a room of my own.

"Upstairs, come with me."

As I trailed behind him up the carpeted steps, I was feeling thankful that I wouldn't be scrubbing the steps on my hands and knees with a mixture of ammonia and vinegar in a metal gallon bean bucket like I had to at Mooseheart.

Flashbacks of scrubbing the hardwood steps in Muncie Hall-where I lived with 20 other six and seven-year old little girls-went through my mind. When it was our turn for the assignment of scrubbing the steps with a toothbrush, we were down on our hands and knees for hours. After that chore, we polished the tiled linoleum floors. The matrons tied rags on our feet and for two hours we skated up and down the long floors-imagining we were on an ice skating rink-until "the floors shined like the top of the Chrysler building." If our work passed inspection, we earned the privilege of watching The Lawrence Welk show. If our work didn't pass inspection, we were sent to bed an hour earlier.

I snapped back to the present when I heard a door slam, but I didn't know where I was or how I got there. I recognized my brother Paul who was showing me around the upstairs apartment where we would be living. There was a living room, kitchen, bathroom, a bedroom for my mom and a bedroom for me. My brothers, Warren, and Bob, would sleep in the attic.

After seeing my bedroom, we went back down stairs and Paul told Dottie we were going downtown. I hopped in the front seat of his 1970 dark green Pontiac and drove to the G.C. Murphy Department store on Erie Avenue to pick out what ever color paint I wanted for my very own bedroom. I chose a gallon of hot pink paint. We returned home and started painting the room. Paul taped off the woodwork with masking tape, and I brushed the walls with the paint. He showed me how to use a small brush for the trim and how to use a roller.

"Paint in one direction so it looks nice when it's done." He instructed me.

After the room was painted, we went down to the Trend Furniture store and bought a box spring and mattress and an unfinished dresser that he stained and varnished for me. Dottie gave me a JC Penney Catalog that was as thick as the Chicago phone book and told me to pick out a bedspread and curtains for the room. I chose a bright, solid yellow bedspread and curtains to match. After the room was all done, Paul remarked: "That room looks snazzy Brat."

For the first time in my life I had my own space and would spend hours in the bedroom listening to 45 records on a portable turntable and writing letters to all my friends in Mooseheart. Except they would never receive them because the dean censored the letters and didn't appreciate me asking how they were doing in the "jail."

My mom got a job working at the dry cleaners in St. Marys because she had experience working in the industrial laundry at Mooseheart. For some reason, I began calling her "Ma" instead of mom.

Before leaving for work in the morning, Ma would have a beer or two. When returning from work in the afternoon, she would have a Seven and Seven; a mixed drink of Seven-up soda and Seagram whiskey.

Ma was a hard worker, but not very thorough. There were always dirty dishes in the sink. She wasn't a neat freak and didn't make me set the table, nor did she insist that I make my bed. She didn't have to. Every morning when I woke up, I made the bed like I was taught to do since I was three years old. I tucked the sheets in tight with sqare triangles at the corners. The blanket needed to be perfectly even on each side of the bed and the bedspread was folded down and then pulled up over the pillow.

On the weekends, Ma took me to auctions to buy items for the kitchen and furniture for the living room. I didn't realize that these items could be bought at stores. One weekend she drove me back to Sharon, Pennsylvania where I was born. It was the first time I was there since my daddy died. We stayed in New Wilmington with her boyfriend Fred, who had Amish folk as neighbors.

Fred was an old man with gray hair and a scruffy beard, who lived in a two-story brick house that smelled old and musty. The kitchen table was covered with newspaper instead of a table cloth. There wasn't any indoor plumbing. The toilet was an outhouse in the backyard. Water had to be pumped from a hand pump and carried inside. I wondered how many other people outside of Mooseheart lived like this.

When I walked up on the concrete porch, he kissed me and stuck his tongue in my mouth. It was wet and disgusting and reeked of Jim Beam Bourbon.

My brothers stored cases of beer in the stone spring house beside the house. Next to the spring house there was a summer kitchen that was used for cooking so the main house didn't get too hot in the summer. I peeked in the window of the summer kitchen and saw a maple corner cabinet that my dad had built before he died. My mom said that belonged to my brother Jack and when he got home from Vietnam he could have it.

Little Amish children, dressed in blue and black clothes, walking barefoot in the lane behind Fred's house caught my eye. I was curious about their lifestyle and wanted to see how they lived. Since they were friends of Fred's, I was able to visit them in their wood frame two story house that was neat and clean.

The woman of the house was ironing clothes with a black iron heated on the wood cook stove. Canning jars of beets, tomatoes, corn and jellies lined wood shelves in the kitchen. The beds were made neatly with beautiful quilts. I thought about asking them if they would like to adopt me. I hoped someday I could live like them.

Ma took me to see all my relatives that hadn't seen me in ten years. When they saw me, they would say "Oh, this is little Jeanette." I wondered what was wrong with them that they couldn't see that I wasn't little anymore.

There were so many contrasts between the relatives on my mother's side. Her younger sister Velma, from whom I had received a card and a five-dollar bill every year for my birthday when I was Mooseheart, dressed in cotton capris and a pressed blouse with creases on the sleeves. Her brown hair was tightly pin curled without one strand of hair out of place. She lived in a brick house in Sharon. The inside of her house looked like the halls in Mooseheart with spotless floors, shiny 1950 style appliances, and neatly pressed drapes in the living room and kitchen windows.

Before we went to Mooseheart, my dad and her husband Al would go fishing and bring all seven of us children to her nice clean house. She said we were a bunch of hoodlums, and tried to make us behave, but couldn't.

Later in my life, Aunt Velma told me "I never approved of your mom's drinking and taking you to stay with that drunk Fred, who was one of the reasons why your father is dead." Fred and my father had been drinking the night of the accident that put my father in the hospital before he died.

Uncle Clem, my mom's older brother, was in a wheelchair with saliva drooling down his face. Uncle Clem had Muscular Dystrophy. His wife Rose took care of him like a little child. The children in the house didn't smile or laugh.

Then there was Ronnie, who my mom said was like her little brother, but she didn't call him my Uncle. He was what I called a tad mentally retarded. He didn't make eye contact or talk to me. He was married to a red-headed woman, and they had a child who was more than a tad retarded. I learned later in life that Ronnie was my mom's sister Regina's child. She was a heavy-set woman and had gotten pregnant out of wedlock when she was fifteen, by a man fifty years older than her; my grandparents raised Ronnie as if he was one of their own.

The only relative I enjoyed visiting was Uncle Henry, my dad's youngest brother. He lived on a farm and raised sheep. When we went to visit him, his wife, Aunt Evelyn, didn't invite us into the house, so we sat outside at the picnic table and visited. I loved the warmth of Uncle Henry's deep voice and his tanned skin reminded me of my daddy. On one of our visits, Uncle Henry took me to see my father's grave at the Hermitage cemetery in Sharon.

I had been there with my mom before, but when I went with Uncle Henry, I broke down and cried for over an hour. The tears wouldn't stop. He held me and let me cry into the shoulder of his flannel shirt for a long time. I never returned to the cemetery again.

We also went to visit my Oma, who now had dementia, and was staying with her adult granddaughter. I was excited to see the grandma that smelled of camphor and gave me black licorice, but she didn't remember me, although when she heard the name Jeanette she perked up. I thought she remembered me, but it was her daughter, Jeanette who she remembered.

On one of the visits "back home," Ma took my brother Warren and me to see the Sharon Lake. Memories of me dressed in hand me down raggedy clothes, romping around barefoot with our pony Bonnie, my cat Tissy and my collie Laddie made me feel as if I were three years old again. I didn't find the visits "back home" very pleasant as I had no way to process the deep sadness and loss. When we got on I-80 to drive back to St. Marys, I returned to feeling like a teen-ager again.

In July, my sister Ginny, her husband and four children, Paul, Dennis, Barby and Tammy, drove to Pennsylvania from Hartford, Connecticut where they were living. They pulled into the driveway in a beat-up station wagon and it didn't look like they had much money. The kids were barefoot and dressed in raggedy clothes.

I hadn't seen her for eight years and felt like she was a stranger. The only thing familiar was how she screamed at the kids. Her and her husband both smoked cigarettes, one right after the other. She was happy to see all her brothers and me again, but no one knew what to talk about.

During the long month of August, I walked by myself to Memorial Park in St. Marys, to swim in the community pool that was located just behind our house. There were two diving boards and a high dive. As I climbed the steps up to the high dive, my head began to throb and I felt as if I was doing a back dive at the Mooseheart swimming pool when I cracked my head open on the diving board.

Unfortunately, the "accident" didn't end in my demise. If I died jumping off the high dive at the community pool it wouldn't be the worst thing that happened to me. Therefore, I had no fear. I numbly dived into the cool water, came up for air, swam to the edge of the pool, got out and walked back to the new house.

Our house was within walking distance of downtown St. Marys. The town, which was called a borough, felt safe with the steeples of churches dotting the neighborhoods. I liked the feeling of walking around freely without a permit to go from one building to the next.

The GC Murphy department store had a little restaurant that served hamburgers and French fries. Down the street was a Widmann's Drug Store that sold Kotex pads and tampons. I didn't like stealing them from Dottie, so I went into Ma's room and took money from her purse so I could get what I needed. I decided to buy tampons, as they would be easier to sneak in the house and hide under my clothes. I had no idea how to use them and didn't have anyone to ask, so I read the directions in the box.

For the most part, I sat up in my room for the next few weeks until school started. I loved looking down at the world, thinking that maybe that's how God looked down from heaven. As I watched the cars go up and down the street, I wondered why he would let people get in car wrecks and die if he was watching them and could stop them. After all he was God.

Even though I had my very own bedroom, I couldn't sleep at night. It was hard for me to get pictures of Mooseheart out of my mind. Especially pictures of how children were treated. I wondered how the little boy who jumped off the red caboose at the playground was doing. I couldn't stop feeling like it was my fault but didn't have anyone to talk to about my experience.

More importantly I didn't have anyone to help me transition from living in an institution to living in the outside world. I was completely on my own and felt as if had been dropped in the middle of the forest. I thought about the childhood story, *Hansel and Gretel* and wondered how they ever found their way out of the woods.

Thankfully, on my journey I found people to help me learn the ropes and make my way in life.

Chapter Eight

For my fourteenth birthday, Ma took me shopping for school clothes downtown in St. Marys on Erie Avenue. Berman's clothing store, was owned by a heavy set Jewish man, who wore dark rimmed glasses and smoked a cigar. Kantars Department Store was a few doors down and sold clothing, patterns and fabric for sewing clothes, along with skeins of yarn, knitting needles, and crochet hooks. Ma said the St. Mary's stores were ritzy and too expensive. Other than going to the clothes store, there wasn't any other celebration for my birthday; no cake, no candles, no presents to unwrap.

Before school started, there was an orientation at the high school I would be attending on the Million Dollar Highway. Ma had to take the day off work for the orientation and complained the whole way to the school about how much money she was losing that day. I wondered how I would get to the school every day when she was working.

The St. Mary's Area High School was only a year old and ten times the size of the small Mooseheart school. There were over three hundred students in the ninth-grade class, versus only thirty students in the eighth-grade class at Mooseheart. As a group of us toured the school I felt as if I was in huge maze and worried how I would ever find my way around the large school with more classrooms than I could count on my fingers.

Some of the other kids seemed to know each other and said they were from the valley. The only valley I had ever heard of was the song *The Harper Valley PTO*. I started singing the song in my head to combat the awkwardness of being with a crowd of people I didn't know. I later learned that kids from the "valley" lived halfway between St. Marys and Du Bois and had attended elementary school in Bennett's Valley, but would now be bussed to St. Mary's for high school.

A girl named Cheryl with long straight brown hair parted down the middle befriended me. She just moved from Buffalo and lived with her grandmother. I wished I had pretty hair and modern clothes like her. The guidance teacher gave us a schedule and told us where we would catch the bus that would take us to school. The bus would pick my brother Warren and me up on the corner of Maurus and North St. Marys Street.

The first day of school was noisy with kids talking and bells ringing. I felt like my head was going to explode. I didn't know how to navigate my way through the hallways to find my classes. The only room I remembered from the orientation was the band room, where I signed up for clarinet lessons. Next to the band room was the art room, where Mr. Slater taught painting and drawing. He had large plastic framed glasses and spoke with a kind, gentle voice and looked like he wouldn't hurt a flea.

I approached him with my schedule and told him I was lost. He asked to look at my schedule. As he walked me to my homeroom class, I felt like I was drowning in a sea of humanity. Everyone else seemed to know what they were doing and where they were going. I just pretended, which would be my way of coping for the next few years. I pretended I knew where I was at. I pretended I was someone I wasn't. I pretended to be like everyone else because I had no idea who I was.

When it was time for lunch, I had to wait in a long line. When it was my turn to pay for lunch, instead of telling the lunch lady that I didn't have any money, I told her I wasn't hungry. There was no one to tell me where to sit. I felt so alone. I saw an empty chair near the window and sat by myself, staring out the window. The next day I told my mom I needed money for lunch. She gave me two dollars and told me it had to last me for a month. I signed up to work in the cafeteria during lunch so I could earn enough money to buy something to eat.

At band practice Mr. Sinibaldi, the band director, was kind and spent extra time giving me lessons on the clarinet. My brother Paul bought me a used clarinet, but I wasn't allowed to practice after school because it squeaked and got on Ma's nerves. I wasn't very good and made the third chair in the clarinet section.

Susan Yonkofsky, who had long dishwater blond hair and played 3rd clarinet, sat next to me during band practice and helped me out when I was lost. During marching band practice, I met a girl named Sally, who was short, had curly hair and wire-framed glasses. She played the flute and would talk to me during breaks.

I was enrolled in the College Prep curriculum and managed A's, and B's in all my classes, including Geometry and Biology. It didn't take long for me to become comfortable with the spaciousness at SMAHS. Not only did I have a little free time to roam the hallways, but my mind opened up to new ideas and concepts.

One of my favorite teachers was Mr. Granche, who taught English. He introduced the class to *The Catcher in the Rye* and *Flowers for Algernon*; books that I would have never been allowed to read in Mooseheart. For the first time in my life, I learned about black people when we read *Nigger* and *Black Like Me*. The library at the school was immense, with an upstairs where I could daydream and learn more about the world.

The students I got to know best were the ones in my homeroom class with last names that began with S through Z. The same kids would be in my homeroom class for the next four years. Cindy Salter, Suzie Tornatore, Doug Wilson, Val Wilson, Amy Yacabucci, Susan Yonkfoski and Irene

Weisner became familiar faces who smiled at me and said hello. They were like a light rain that was softening my heart and easing my transition into the free world.

The girls in school dressed nicely. Their hair was clean and parted down the middle. Mine was greasy and wavy. I began using scotch tape at night to tame the waves. The girls carried purses and wore makeup, bell bottoms and tight-knit midriff shirts. Some of the girls wore short dresses with matching underwear that were called sizzlers. I began to take notice of what kind of clothes I needed to wear to fit in.

After school, when I got home, Ma would be laying on the couch drinking beer and reading The Daily Press. Paul and Dottie both worked the 3-11 shift and my brother Bob worked 11-7 shift at Carbon City and slept during the day. There wasn't anything for me to do but go to my room and write letters to my old friends at Mooseheart. Sometimes I wished I was back there again. I missed the girls who called me Van. I felt like a lonely little puppy who was taken away from it's litter mates.

Dottie noticed how withdrawn I was, so she surprised me with a black and white rat terrier dog that I named Jo-Jo. That was my nickname before I went to Mooseheart, because my brother Warren couldn't pronounce my name. I didn't like the dog, but Dottie picked it out for me and I didn't want to hurt her feelings. It was an older dog, it's breath smelled and it barked a lot, but it was better than coming home to a lonely house after school. I never had a pet before and didn't know to take it outside to go the bathroom. It messed in the house and made my room smell.

Two days a week, there was marching band practice after school. The marching band played at the football games during half-time at Berwind Park behind the middle school. A girl named Cindy Tettis who played the flute would come over and talk to me when I would be standing alone. She lived behind the middle school on Rock Street. The night air at the football games was cold.

Parents of the other kids brought them coats, blankets, and hot chocolate to drink during the game. I sat alone shivering like a lonely leaf, barely staying afloat on a cold pond. Most of the other kids had parents who were band boosters and lived in Leave It To Beaver houses, leaving me feeling as I was some kind of freak.

When October arrived, I was in awe when the leaves turned from green to stunning shades of red, yellow, orange and brown. I had never seen such beauty in Illinois, where only a few trees dropped rust color leaves. I enjoyed the morning bus ride to school when the air was cool and crisp, and frost covered the ground.

I signed up for a class trip to see the musical Jesus Christ Superstar in Pittsburgh. It was my first time attending a live rock concert and going to Pittsburgh. The thrill of the loud music and the crowd of people was energizing. I related to Jesus who seemed like an outcast.

In late fall, my brother Bob thought I should go hunting and told me that I needed to take a hunter's safety course so I could get my deer license. I passed the course. He took me out hunting for squirrels in the fall. I screamed when he shot a squirrel out of a tree. I told him I didn't want to shoot animals. He told me I was prissy just like Dottie, and didn't take me hunting anymore.

When winter arrived, Paul took me snowmobiling with him. I rode on the back of his Ski-Doo and enjoyed being outside in the snow. He bought me snowmobile boots, a black and yellow Ski-Doo jacket and snow pants. Snowmobiling on the weekends gave me something to look forward to. The excitement of going fast made me feel alive.

Dottie and Paul went out of their way to make Christmas special for Warren and me, since it was our first Christmas out of Mooseheart. We went Christmas shopping to the Monroeville Mall in Pittsburgh. Paul bought me a vinyl bright yellow beanbag chair to match my room and Dottie bought me enough material from Kantars to make a quilt that I planned on sewing by hand, just like the Amish.

Paul bought Dottie a new appliance, called a microwave oven. For Christmas, they cooked a ham in less than an hour. The dinner didn't have all the trimmings like cranberries, olives, and mints, like Mooseheart, but we were free and happy. Everyone was drinking booze and no one cared that I drank sloe gin and grapefruit juice that tasted like Kool-Aid.

After drinking a few glasses I became dizzy and could barely walk up to the steps to the apartment. When I got to my room, I threw up all over my bed. I never drank sloe gin again.

The next summer my brothers Bill and Bob took me boating to the East Branch Dam on a motorboat they bought together. On the weekends, we packed up a couple of tents, some food, and coolers of beer to go camping.

I was fourteen now and that must have been old enough to drink because they would let me drink the "SHITS" beer. It was Schmidts, but if you took every other letter out then it spelled shits, and that's what my brothers called it because it gave you diarrhea when you drank it.

The lukewarm beer made me gag, but I drank it anyway because there wasn't anything else to drink. Gary, a short, stout boy with blonde hair that worked with my brothers at Carbon City, started to join us. Since he couldn't swim and was afraid of water, he wore an orange life vest and drove the boat while we water skied.

My brothers could ski on one ski and go back and forth across the waves. It took me a few times to get up on the skis, but I got the hang of it without too much trouble.

Dottie helped me pick out a bright orange bikini with an orange jacket from the JC Penney Catalog. I would sunbathe on the dock for hours until my skin was as red as a lobster. Gary told me how sexy I looked in the bikini and began talking to me. He asked if I would like to go to the drive-in with him sometime.

I said "Sure."

He said, "Do you want to ask your mom and then let me know?"

"She doesn't give a shit what I do," I replied

"I will pick you up next Saturday night at 6:00. Would you like me to give you a ride home tonight?"

I was more than happy to get away from my brothers as they were driving me crazy with their loud talking and drinking so much beer. After we packed up the tents, I put my backpack of clothes in the back seat of Gary's 1970 forest green Ford Torino.

The loud glass pack muffler rumbled as he revved the engine and drove slowly out of the campground. Once we hit the pavement, he shifted quickly into fifth gear, and we were flying around the curves of the back-road from East Branch Dam to St. Marys. The weekend didn't come fast enough. On Friday night, Gary called me from Carbon City, the powdered metal factory where he worked second shift from 3-11 pm.

"Hi, Jeanette. I was calling to see if you were still going with me to the drive-in tomorrow night."

"Sure,"

"OK. I'll be there at 6:00."

At 6:00 I heard the familiar loud sound of the muffler pull into the paved driveway next to the house. My mom was in her bedroom reading a *True Story* magazine. As I walked down the first three steps and opened the paned glass door, she hollered "Where are you going?"

I sped up my pace as I hollered back that we were going to the drive-in.

Gary was dressed in a pair of creased blue jeans and a burgundy and white checkered short sleeve dress shirt that was unbuttoned at the collar. His long blonde shoulder length hair was damp and parted to the right side. The car smelled like leather and floor mats were as shiny as a crow's feathers. The shiny mag aluminum wheels reflected the pine trees that flanked the driveway.

I opened the passenger door of the "muscle car" and slid into the front seat. With his right hand on the shifter and his left hand propped on the steering wheel, he asked me "What time do you have to be home?"

"My mom doesn't give a shit."

"Curfew is at midnight, so I'll have you home before then."

Before going to see the movie, we stopped at the Little Skipper Drive-In Restaurant on the Million Dollar Highway, located about a mile before the entrance to the high school I attended.

The restaurant reminded me of the Dog N' Suds in Aurora, Illinois where Paul had gallon glass jugs refilled with root beer when I visited him and Dottie in Rockford. He would buy me a root beer float that I would slowly slurp through the straw, hoping it would take us longer to get back to the hall at Mooseheart.

Gary ordered both of us a hamburger, an order of fries and a coke. A girl in a short skirt and white apron brought the food out to the car and set it on a tray that attached to the door of the car. I sipped the coke slowly.

After eating, we drove up the road a few miles to the drive-in theater to see The Poseidon Adventure. Going to a drive-in movie was a brand-new experience for me. When we got to the drive-in, Gary parked the car and attached the speaker to the door of the car. He told me to slide closer to him. I straddled the Hurst five gear shifter and sat next to him with my hands tucked between my legs. He put his right arm around me.

I couldn't remember the last time someone touched me and wasn't sure I liked the feel of his hand touching the skin of my bare upper arm. I wished I would have worn long sleeves or brought a jacket. He pulled a pack of red and white Marlboro cigarettes out of his shirt pocket and lit up a cigarette and passed it to me. "Do you want a drag?" I took a long, deep drag of the cigarette that made me feel dizzy and lightheaded.

After the movie, we cruised up and down the Million Dollar Highway a few times before he took me home. After he had pulled into the driveway, he turned off the car engine so it wouldn't wake anyone up. As I was getting out of the car he asked, "Would you like to come up to my parent's house for dinner on Sunday? My mom would like to meet you."

Without hesitation, I said "Sure."

"Don't you want to ask your mom first?"

"I told you, she doesn't give a shit."

"We eat at noon, so I'll pick you up at 11:30."

"Okay. See you then."

After he dropped me off, I crept up the apartment steps so my mom wouldn't hear me. The wood floor creaked as I walked to my bedroom. Just as I was about to open the door to my room, she hollered, "Where were you?"

"I told you I went to the drive-in." I went into my bedroom, shut the door and slid Melanie Safka's 45 album out of the cover and held it by the edges, setting it gently on my portable turntable. I plugged in the large headphones so I couldn't hear if she tried to talk to me again and fell asleep listening to the song, *A Brand New Pair of Roller Skates*.

The next day, Gary pulled into the driveway on a 650 Honda motorcycle. I put on a helmet and got on the back of the bike. We drove up to his brick, two-story house only a few blocks away on Mark Street. After getting off the bike, he walked me up to the back porch where his dad, dressed in a white undershirt and pressed dress pants, was sitting on a glider.

"Dad, this is Jeanette."

With a King Edward cigar hanging out of his mouth, he said "I know your brothers Paul and Bob. They told me about you."

"Bud" worked with my brothers at Carbon City. In fact, he was their boss. I wondered what they told him about me.

Gary opened the screen door for me and I walked into the house that felt like a real home with frilly kitchen curtains and throws rugs on the floor. The smell of homemade food made my stomach growl. Polka music was playing on the transistor radio.

"Hi, mom. This is Jeanette."

Mona, a short, plump woman with short, tightly curled hair and a smile that melted my heart was bent over pulling a pan of Shake N' Bake chicken out of the oven. "Nice to meet you, Jeanette."

Gary's two sister's Patty and Cindy were sitting in the living room watching TV. The room was nicely decorated with autumn colored shag wall to wall carpeting, two upholstered chairs, a coffee table with doilies and a candy dish filled with Smarties. I recognized Cindy from my home-room class and band. Both of the girls said hi.

When we went into the living room, Gary ordered Cindy to move out of the chair where she was sitting so he could sit down. She did. Then he told Patty to change the station on the TV. She got up and turned the channel for him.

I stood in the doorway between the kitchen and the living room for a minute and then turned around to the kitchen. Bud came in from outside and started mashing the potatoes.

"Mrs. Salter, do you need any help with dinner?"

His mom didn't answer me right away. She looked at me inquisitively and then asked, "Would you like to carry in the dish of corn to the table?"

She handed me the vegetable dish and directed me to the dining room table that was formally set for Sunday dinner and followed behind me carrying a large bowl of mashed potatoes, telling me I could sit next to Gary. A bird cage with a canary hung in the corner of the room. I felt as if I was on the Leave it to Beaver show, eating in a real house with a real family for the first time in my life.

After two helpings of mashed potatoes and chicken, his mom commented on what a good appetite I had. Other than that, there wasn't much conversation during the dinner.

After everyone was finished eating, Patty and Cindy left to hang out with some of their friends. I wished I had friends to hang out with. While Gary was watching football, I asked his mom where the dish towel was. She took a neatly folded floral terrycloth drying towel out of the drawer next to silverware drawer and handed it to me. After I had dried the dishes, I stacked them on the table. When the dishes were done, she thanked me for helping.

While pouring two glasses of instant iced tea, she asked if I wanted to sit out on the back porch. We sat on the glider and she talked about all the chores she did that week and told me about the two little girls, Renee and Tanya that she babysat. She also told me how she and Bud waited ten years after they were married to have Gary and then it was another four years before they had Cindy because Gary wouldn't sleep in his own bed. She went on to tell me that when Patty was born with a broken collar bone, Bud sat and rocked her for hours and hours.

I sat and listened to her talk and talk thankful that she didn't expect me to talk. Gary came out about an hour later and asked if I wanted to go for a ride. His mom asked him if my mom minded me riding on a motorcycle.

"Nah, she doesn't care," I said.

"You be careful, Gary" his mom chided.

During the last semester of tenth grade, I was called to the guidance office. I thought I had done something wrong, but the guidance counselor told me that I qualified to attend a six-week summer Upward Bound program for low-income families at Lock Haven. He handed me a manila envelope with papers that needed to be signed by my mother.

When I asked my mother to sign the papers, without even looking at them, she told me we didn't have money to send me to a university and tossed them on the floor along with the Daily Press that she read each day.

I salvaged the envelope from the stack of papers and waited until the weekend when Dottie was home from work to ask her to sign the papers. When I told Dottie about the program at school and what Ma said, her smile turned to a frown. I asked if she would sign the papers for me since her name was also Dorothy VanZanten.

She read over the papers and said, "Sure, I'll sign them. It doesn't look like it will cost anything for you to go. Paul and I will give you spending money." I returned the papers to the guidance office and was happy when the counselor looked over the papers and said everything was good to go. He told me the date and said that I would have to find someone to drive me to Lock Haven.

Jack returned from Viet Nam in February of 1973. He now had a girlfriend named Connie, who he had met while working in Southern Illinois before he left for Vietnam. Connie wrote letters to him while he was overseas and the two of them began dating when he returned to the States.

While on leave, he came back to St. Marys at the same time I needed a ride to Lock Haven. On his way back to Fort Bragg, he drove me down to Lock Haven in his blue and black Opal and dropped me off in front of the building where I needed to register.

I carried my sleeping bag and the duffel bag of clothes up the concrete steps. When I opened the heavy doors, I was greeted by a large black man, dressed in bell bottoms, a t-shirt, and sneakers. He had large afro hair and a smile that stretched from one ear to the other. As he grabbed the duffel bag that was slung over my shoulder he introduced himself.

"Hey, my name is Terrell. Welcome to Upward Bound." Terrell was the first black man I saw in person.

"What's your name and where are you from, young lady?"

"I'm Jeanette, and I live in St. Mary's."

"Cool, we are glad to have you here. I'll help you find your dorm and get registered."

I looked around the large room and felt relaxed to see a man with long hair sitting on a sofa in the lounge area strumming on a guitar.

Terrell gave me a paper with a room number and told me what floor I would be staying on. I told him I was lost so he hollered at a black girl named Marianne to help me find my way.

Marianne swaggered over to where Terrell and I were standing and said "Sure."

She tried to help me carry my sleeping bag, but I held on to it and said: "No, I can carry my stuff." I had read about slaves and didn't want anyone being my slave.

As we climbed two flights of steps to our dormitory, Marianne hummed out loud and gave all the other kids high fives as they passed each other.

"Here, this is your room, right across from mine." When she opened the door, I was relieved to see a white girl with long blonde hair hanging up a poster of Robert Redford above her bed. She introduced me to Pam and said, "Jeanette is your roomie."

I put my stuff on the empty bed next to a window and thanked Marianne for helping me.

"No problem, girlfriend. We're having a party in my room tonight. Why don't you come on over for a while?"

When we all gathered in the cafeteria for supper, I recognized some of the kids from St. Mary's High School and didn't feel so alone. Monty Cousins was a year ahead of me and had the prettiest blue eyes. He recognized me and waved.

After supper, I hung out in the lounge area with Pam and some other kids, where we sang folk songs to the hippie's guitar music. After the sun went down, we returned to the dorm.

Unfamiliar music with a heavy rhythmic beat shook the floors and blared from the open bedroom doors. A sweet- smelling odor swirled in the air. I knew it wasn't the smell of cigarettes, and it certainly didn't smell like food. When I walked by Marianne's bedroom, she was sitting on her bed smoking a pipe that didn't look like the pipe that Mr. Gulley smoked. Smoke billowed out of her mouth and into the air.

"Hey girlfriend, come take a hit of this shit."

I didn't want to be rude and tell her no, so I walked over to where she was sitting. Marianne handed me the glass pipe with water. I took a long deep hit. "Hold it in your lungs for a little bit," she instructed.

After letting out a long breath, I looked into the bowl of the pipe and saw a small piece of black charcoal. Acting cool, and talking like a black girl, I asked, "What is this shit?"

"It's some good hash."

The floor beneath my feet felt like it was moving and I started to feel dizzy. A tall black girl came out of the bathroom with a towel wrapped around her slender body.

"Hey Brenda, this is Jeanette. She's in the room across the hall from us, and is really cool."

Brenda took the pipe and took a long hit and handed it to me again. This time I pretended to take a hit and passed the pipe back to Marianne. The loud music felt like it was pounding inside of my head.

I told the girls that I was tired and needed to sleep. I found my way back to my room and crashed on the bed that was spinning. When I awoke the next morning, I didn't remember what happened the night before or what I should be doing at the present moment.

Pam told me that we had to be down in the cafeteria for breakfast by 8:00. I threw on the same blue jean shorts and halter top I wore the night before and we walked to the cafeteria together.

After breakfast, we were given a schedule of activities for the day that we would follow for the next three weeks. My schedule included a photography class, music theory, and volleyball. In the photography class, we were given 35 mm cameras and learned how to develop film. We had plenty of free time to roam the campus and find our way to downtown Lock Haven where we bought hoagies and soda.

In the evenings, we attended open air folk and rock concerts where college kids openly smoked cigarettes and pot. On weekends, we went on educational field trips to different state parks, including Watkin's Glenn in New York State. Watkin's Glen is not only famous for car races but for a stunning gorge that is creviced between two mountains.

For the first time in my life, I felt true peace as I walked up the stone steps, and under waterfalls, with the sound of water rushing over the rocks that emptied into Seneca Lake. I had been to Lake Michigan when I lived in Illinois, but it was polluted and dirty; Seneca Lake was clean and placid.

The kids in photography club were armed with cameras and were instructed to take photographs of the landscape and any other interesting sights. I snapped a black and white picture of an old man sitting on a park bench and received an A for the assignment. I enjoyed taking photographs and felt connected to the popular song, *Kodachrome* by Paul Simon.

It didn't take much for me to bond with the girls on my dorm floor. I felt as if I had known them forever. The living situation reminded me of Mooseheart and if felt good to have a sense of belonging. One of the girls was from Emporium, a town near St. Marys. When I told her I was dating Gary Salter, she said she knew him. I didn't realize she was in touch with him and would tell him everything that went on at Lock Haven.

I preferred spending time with the black kids. They taught me how to corn braid hair and turned me on to Billy Preston music. Even though I didn't care for all the pot smoking as it made me tired, I faked taking tokes from the pipe when it was passed to me.

Marianne confided in me that she was pregnant and would be having a baby that winter. When she told me, I said, "That's cool." She said, "You are the first person that didn't call me stupid for having the baby." Marianne talked about Mount Union, the little town she was from and told me that even though she was at the top of her class and this was her senior year, she was planning on getting married to her boyfriend in the fall and asked me to be in her wedding.

After three weeks at Lock Haven, over the Fourth of July weekend, we had a break. Gary drove down to pick me up. I was excited for him to meet my new friends, but when I introduced him to the black counselor Terrell, he rudely blew cigarette smoke in his face and walked away.

On the drive home, he complained about my nigger friends and said I wasn't going back for the next three weeks.

The minute I got back to my house at St. Mary's, Ma started talking about the niggers down there. I told her to shut up and that in the fall I was going to Mount Union to be in my friend Marianne's wedding.

"You aren't going to any nigger town, and you aren't going back to Lock Haven."

I shut myself in my room for the whole weekend and didn't get out of bed for two days. When Gary called, I told him I was sick.

Ma got worried and called Dottie. When I went down to talk to Dottie, I told her I was tired and just wanted to sleep all the time. She made an appointment with a Dr. Valigorsky in Weedville and took me to the appointment.

After some bloodwork, he diagnosed me with mononucleosis. No one would take me back to Lock Haven, but my sleeping bag and some of my clothes were still there, so on a weekend when I was feeling a little better, Gary agreed to take me back down.

The drive down felt longer than driving from Illinois to Pennsylvania. When we arrived at the campus, I told him to stay in the car while I ran in and got my stuff.

All the kids were happy to see me and asked why I didn't come back. I told them about being sick. As I was getting my stuff out of my dorm room, Marianne came into the room with tears in her eyes. "Jeanette, I've been so worried about you." She gave me a warm hug and whispered in my ear, "I missed having someone to talk to."

When we wiped the tears from our eyes, she asked me if I was still going to be in her wedding. I didn't have the heart to tell her that my mom didn't like niggers, so just shook my head no. She handed me a color senior class picture and told me to keep in touch.

The next week Gary took me to the drive-in and he gave me his large brass class ring with a large ruby stone from Cameron County High School Class of 1971. The ring was too big for my thin fingers, so I put it on my thumb until I was able to buy some angora yarn to wrap it, just like all the other girls who had boyfriends did.

Gary started going camping with us overnight at the East Branch Dam. My brothers got kicked out of the camping area for drinking too much, so they bought two tents to haul across the dam in the boat loaded with coolers of beer and some food. There weren't any bathroom facilities, running water or electricity. Gary didn't have a tent, so he slept out by the fire.

One night when it was raining, he asked to come in my tent. I said OK. He laid down beside me and during the middle of the night when everyone else was sleeping he started to touch me. I didn't know I had a voice to say no.

There wasn't anything in particular that I liked about Gary, except his mom. Every time I went up to his house she was just so nice to me. Sunday dinner at his house became a ritual. The home cooked meals of scalloped potatoes and ham, roast beef with potatoes and carrots, city chicken made from ground veal, meatloaf, and boiled pot pie noodles in ham broth were delicious and stuck with me through the week when I didn't eat much.

On weekends, Gary and I would go in the basement of the house that was fixed up like a family room, unlike the stone, dirty basement of my house. The floor was carpeted, and there were chairs, a television, a pool table and a bar with shelves stocked full of whiskey and a keg of Straub's beer on tap. Gary started to ask me up to his house on Saturdays. When no one was home, I asked where everyone was at.

He told me his mom didn't drive, and his dad took her shopping to Bradford, Olean or DuBois on the weekend. He suggested we go up to his bedroom to listen to music on his Pioneer stereo with a turntable, an eight-track tape player and large speakers that sat on corner shelves. I thought we were just going to listen to music, but it always ended up being more than that.

In late summer, my brother Paul found me a babysitting job taking care of three kids that were just a few years younger than me. Their dad worked with Paul at Carbon City. The kids lived a mile or so out of town on Washington Street, so I rode my bike out to watch them until the mom came home from bartending.

Then I would ride my bike home in the dark until one of Gary's friends, a creepy, older guy named Cecil, who had a gas station on Brusselles Street stopped to give me a ride. He said I could put my bike in the back of his truck. When I told him no, he told me he would be at the house where I was babysitting the next day.

I was nervous and afraid all day. That night, when it was time for me to go home from babysitting, to distract him, I called the garage and said there was a wreck out on the Million Dollar highway. I told Gary his friend was stalking me and thankfully it came to an end.

By the time September came, I was ready to start school again, but this time found myself with a different group of kids than those who were in the band. I gravitated towards the kids who were drinking and smoking cigarettes in the lavatories as they were accepting of me.

Many of them came from "broken" homes and didn't have a mom and dad who lived together. We met in the bathroom during lunch breaks or during study halls to smoke.

I quickly became friends with a girl nicknamed Bum. She was petite with long blonde hair parted down the middle and wore gold wire rim

John Lennon glasses and wore bib overalls, flannel shirts and tan work boots. I liked her style. She transferred to the public school because she got kicked out of Elk County Catholic.

I asked where she got her clothes and she told me a men's store in St. Marys and invited me to go with her sometime. When we went into the old store there weren't clothes hanging on racks, but boxes stacked to the ceiling and clothes piled on the floor. Bum knew the old man at the store. With my babysitting money, I bought a pair of bib overalls, men's work boots and a flannel shirt to wear to school, all for ten dollars.

Bum smoked pot and knew who to buy it from. She taught me how to roll joints with Zig Zag papers and told me to be careful someone didn't sell me bags of oregano instead of pot and to never pay more than ten bucks for an ounce.

On the weekend, she invited me to a party at an old two-story house with no electric. The only light was from burning candles. There was no place to sit except on bare mattresses. She introduced me to her friends, Dave and Woody. They were tripping on acid and drinking Boon Mountain Wine. I felt uncomfortable and told her I had to get home.

She also introduced me to her friend Vicky who had an apartment in downtown St. Marys. Whenever Vicky needed anything from the store, she told Bum to go to GC Murphys for her. Since I didn't know Vicky very well, I tagged along with Bum and was surprised when she didn't pay for anything. She shoplifted everything and anything, believing she was like Robin Hood stealing from the rich and giving to the poor.

Before long I was shoplifting right along with her. She taught me how to slide albums under a large coat. I started to feel guilty and was afraid of getting caught, so I tried to avoid going places with her on weekends.

Vicky was a year ahead of me in school, but I started running into her in the lavatory before classes. When she came into school in the morning and didn't have time to wash her hair, she would use PSSSSSST dry shampoo that she got from her mom who was a mortician in town. She was dating Tom Uhl, Gary's first cousin and invited me to party with them. One day out of the blue, she asked me if I would be interested in a job.

I asked, "Doing what?"

"There are these two little girls I've been babysitting. You babysit their cousins. I thought you would like my job."

The two girls lived only a block from my house, and I liked the idea of not having to ride my bike home every night when it was dark. Also, I wanted Vicky to be my friend and like me, so I agreed. I made a buck an hour watching two kids.

Tammy and Wendy Snyder were good little girls, aged six and seven. Their mom, Sandy worked second shift, and their dad, Ray went fishing and worked for the ambulance in the evenings. Sandy made fried Spam, potatoes and a vegetable nearly every night and left it on the stove for the girl's supper. I went across the street to Vito's and got a heated hoagie to eat.

Between spending the weekends at Gary's and babysitting during the week, I wasn't home much at all. My mom's boyfriend Arnie, from Illinois, came to visit a few times and stayed overnight, sleeping in my mom's room. They didn't close the door and when I came home at night, I felt uncomfortable, knowing they were in the next room, sleeping together.

As much as I liked the babysitting job, sometimes it was a little scary. The dad would bring his friends who were older men into the house and they would fry walleye fish for supper.

One of the guys, nicknamed Statesy, was an old, fat man with a bald head and glasses. In a deep, wheezy voice he asked: "Would you like me to give you a ride home?"

I didn't say no because at Mooseheart, we were never allowed to say no to anyone, especially an adult. He opened the passenger door of the big car and I got in without thinking that I didn't even know this guy. On the way home, when he didn't turn down the street where I lived to take me home I asked: "Where are we going?"

With a scary chuckle in his voice, he said "Oh, for a little ride."

He headed out of town toward Emporium on Route 120.

"I'm going to show you where I live."

As he was driving, he reached down and unbuckled his pants and popped out his dick. I started screaming as loud as I could. "Take me home right now."

He kept driving. I screamed, "If you don't turn around and take me home right now, I'm jumping out of this car." Thank God, the old car didn't have electric door locks. I pulled the handle and started to open the door. He put on the turn signal and turned the car around.

"What's wrong with you? I was just having some fun." I held onto the door so it didn't fly open and wouldn't talk to him the whole way back to town. I started singing songs in my head and then felt myself floating above the car. He never came back to where I babysat again.

I did okay with grades in tenth grade but wasn't as interested in school. I started to find trouble, without too much effort. A group of kids decided to have a walk out, and I jumped right on the band wagon ending up with two days in-school suspension.

Despite getting in trouble, I was beginning to fit in at school. One day in February, a girl who was in the band came up to me and asked, "Are you Jeanette Van Zanten?"

"Yeah, why?"

"I went to district band this year in Williamsport."

I tried out for district band but didn't make it. I wanted to say, "Aren't you hot shit?" but didn't. Instead, I said "So."

"I stayed with a family, and they have a foster girl that knows you. Her name is Mimi Maly."

My mouth about dropped to the floor. I couldn't believe it. "You saw my friend Mimi Maly? You didn't see Mimi. She lives in Illinois. You are shitting me."

"No, really I did. She told me to give you this," and handed me a folded-up piece of notebook paper with Mimi's name and a phone number.

"Thanks," I replied as I shoved it in the back pocket of my jeans.

Mimi was the little girl that had open heart surgery when we were in Muncie Hall at Mooseheart. As soon as I arrived at the house where I was babysitting, I called the phone number, even though it was a long-distance call. When someone answered the phone, I recognized Mimi's voice right away. "Hi Mimi, this is Van. What the hell are you doing in Williamsport?"

"I got kicked out of Mooseheart."

"No shit? What for?"

"Jerry Haskell and I got caught making out."

"You only live a few hours from St. Marys. Do you want to visit me?"

"My foster parents said I can take the bus to see you."

"When?"

"Next weekend?"

"Really?"

"I already checked it out. I can get a bus into DuBois if someone can pick me up."

"Let me ask my boyfriend."

"That would be groovy."

"I can't wait to see you, Mimi."

The next day Gary was out in front of the high school waiting to give me a ride home before he went to work in the afternoon. When I got in the car I couldn't wait to ask him if he would drive to Dubois that weekend to pick up my friend Mimi.

"Who's Mimi?" he asked?

"She's my friend from Mooseheart."

"She's coming all the way from Mooseheart?"

"No, she got kicked out. She's living in Williamsport, but is going to take a bus here to see me."

"Sure, I'll pick her up."

That weekend Gary picked me up early and we drove to the bus station in DuBois. I was so happy to see Mimi. We spent the weekend together reminiscing about Mooseheart. She told me how nice her foster parents were to her. We stayed up at Gary's house most of the weekend. Gary's mom made us pizza and bought us pop and ice cream. It was a fun time, except I was quite sad when she had to leave.

Seeing Mimi again reminded me of Mooseheart. I couldn't move forward while looking backwards, so didn't stay in touch with her.

I didn't find her until thirty years later when she was living in Georgia. We talked on the phone a few times and I tried real hard to stay in touch, but she quit answering the phone when I called.

A few years later, I became friends with her sister Karen on Facebook. She was living in West Virginia and we met at a Mother Earth Fair in Seven Springs. We were both happy to see each other, but while we had lunch she talked about all the sexual abuse that took place at Mooseheart. It was a lot for me to process and I felt overwhelmed with her stories. We haven't been in touch since.

Chapter Nine

Before Christmas of 1973, there was enough snow for snowmobiling. Paul surprised me with an early Christmas present from Rudy's Saw Shop in Johnsonburg; a brand-new Elan Ski-Do snowmobile.

Every weekend, we went sledding until the day a group of guys who worked with Paul went with us to Twin Lakes State Park near Wilcox, Pennsylvania. A guy named Smokey who worked in the oven room at Carbon City joined us. He was thin and tall, with shoulder length, brown wavy hair and wore raggedy blue jeans and a grey t-shirt under a snowmobile suit that was zipped up halfway. I thought he looked like a Viet Nam draft dodger.

Gary picked Smokey up at his house on North Michael Street that was less than a block from my house on Parade Street. Together they loaded his purple and black Polaris on the back of the trailer next to Gary's sled. They drove to Twin Lakes together in Gary's winter car, a beat up 1967 Ranchero. I rode over with my brother Paul.

After everyone unloaded their sleds from the trailers and put on their helmets, one by one we primed the sled engines and pulled the starter cords. The smell of gasoline permeated the air. By the time the six or seven snowmobiles were all running, they sounded like a pack of angry wolves. Everyone agreed to meet back at the parking lot at 4:00 p.m.

We followed each other in a single line through the wooded park with trees laden with sparkling snow. Paul led the pack. As we navigated through the wooded forest, crossing creeks and bridges, it wasn't long before we lost sight of each other. My snowmobile had a smaller engine and I couldn't keep up with the pack. Smokey was just ahead of me and kept me in eyeshot, frequently looking over his shoulder to check on me. The other guys would stop every once in awhile for a cigarette break, and wait for us to catch up.

After three hours of riding we headed down a steep hill returning to our starting point. At one point, I was alone on the icy road and could no longer hear the buzz of Smokey's sled ahead of me. The sun was setting behind the mountain. I could feel the temperature dropping. Fear set in and my arms began to quiver. The more nervous I became the slower I went not taking my eyes off the road in front of me. When I heard the rumble of the other sleds, I relaxed and was happy to be back with the pack.

When we returned to the parking lot Smokey wasn't there. Paul loaded my sled on the trailer. I sat in Paul's car warming up while the guys drank a few beers. I heard someone ask about Smokey. Did he break down or get lost? When he didn't return, we all decided to go back looking for him. Paul told me to ride on the back of his sled as he didn't want to leave me alone in the parking lot. As the sleds crept up the hill, their headlights bobbed up and down like fireflies in the night. It wasn't long before we spotted a sled that had wrecked into a tree with Smokey lying beside it.

When I got off Paul's snowmobile, I saw that Smokey's head was disjointed from his body. His face was blue and pasty looking. I knew he was dead. I started screaming and crying, "He can't be dead, he can't be dead." Boogie, a short small guy and my brother Bob, hopped on their sleds and drove back down the mountain to call for help.

I stood there shivering to death. I curled up my fingers into the palm of my hands to keep them warm. All of us were frozen. No one knew what to do or say. The silence of the night was deafening. We all just stood there and stared at the dead body.

I felt a presence descend from the night sky that brought peace to my aching heart, that was now frozen solid. An angel came and said his name was Michael. He lifted Smokey up and carried him upward to the dark night sky that was now sparkling with stars.

The sirens and the blue and red emergency lights of the emergency vehicles that were crawling up the hill brought me back to reality. When the ambulance arrived Paul said "C'mon Brat get on the back of my sled." Paul started up the engine on his sled and I saddled the black leather seat and wrapped my arms around his waist. I prayed that Paul would drive slowly so we didn't hit a tree and die going down the mountain. I felt a huge disconnect take place on the ride back. The beauty of the winter night with snow laden on the evergreen branches conflicted with the hurt and loss of seeing someone's life disappear right before my eyes. I couldn't handle the conflict. If this is what happened when someone was having fun, I didn't want to ever want to have fun again.

When we returned to the parking lot, Paul turned on the motor of his green Pontiac and told me to get in to warm up while he finished loading the sleds. Just as I turned on the radio WKBI was playing the words to a familiar song, "We had fun, we had seasons in the sun." I finished the song, "We had fun, we had season in the snow. Now it is time for you to go."

The next day I was in my upstairs bedroom, staring out the window when I saw a cop car pull in the driveway. I crept down the steps and cracked open the wood door at the top of the steps that separated the two apartments of the duplex. I listened as Paul answered the door. The cop asked him, "Were you snowmobiling at Twin Lakes yesterday when Robert Gausman was killed?"

Paul slid his hands in the pocket of his pants. "Yeah, what about it?"

"You left the scene before the coroner arrived."

"I had to get my little sister home."

After hearing those words, I slowly pulled the door shut and ran to my room. I hid in the closet fearing that someone would discover that Smokey's death was my fault.

I hadn't been to a funeral since my father died on November 6th in 1960 when I was three years old. When my dad died, I wasn't tall enough to reach the casket. I stood on my tip toes to see him, lying in a long silvery box, lined with white satin, wearing a suit and tie. I wondered who he was with his black curly hair, graying at the edges, smoothed down and combed to the side. Why wasn't his hair tousled and why wasn't he dressed in his overalls that smelled of the earth, instead of the pretty flowers that smelled like perfume?

"Wake up Daddy. Wake up." I whined.

Suddenly, my thirteen-year old brother Bill came up from behind and grabbed me. He picked me up and said "He won't wake up. He's dead." He grabbed my hand tightly by the wrist and made me touch his cold hand that felt like stone.

I wriggled out of Bill's hands and said, "Leave me alone, leave me alone. I want my Daddy to wake up."

When I went to Smokey's funeral I felt so small. I yearned to say the same thing to Smokey but choked on the words and finally swallowed them. I felt as if I was tagged in the childhood game Statue where I wasn't allowed to move or talk.

Smokey's thin framed mother was heartbroken. I recognized his sister Pauline who went to my school. She had a tissue in her hand and kept wiping her eyes, saying, "Bobby said he would never live to be twenty-one years old and he didn't. He was such a dare devil. He died doing what he wanted to do."

As people milled around the funeral home, I heard my brothers and some guys from Carbon City say that Smokey had talked about killing himself. I didn't know if Smokey's sled hit a patch of ice and wrecked or if he killed himself? I felt like a bad luck charm. My dad died after getting in a car wreck and now Smokey died after getting in a snowmobile wreck. I heard someone else say that he was probably turning around to make sure I was behind him and his sled went over the edge of the ravine. The accident was my fault. I had to hide the guilt, so I refused to cry. I vowed never to get back on a snowmobile again and didn't for many, many years.

I wondered about a God that would on one hand answer my prayers to get out of Mooseheart but on the other hand, let a young man die while having fun. I wasn't sure I wanted to believe in God as I couldn't figure him out. I believed God existed, but personally didn't believe that he gave a shit about people. I wouldn't talk to God anymore, not for a long time anyway.

When I returned to school after the accident, nothing seemed familiar. I felt like a different person starting school all over again. I barely recognized my name when the teacher called roll call in home room. I wanted to tell the teacher that my name was Michael instead of Jeanette. I didn't want to be a girl anymore. I wanted to be one of the guys. I had a hard time completing my homework. I started getting high in the parking lot before school. More than once we were late for our 1st period class, so I started writing tardy excuses, signing my mom's name.

In speech class I had to get up in front of the class and talk about something. I didn't know what to do, so I pulled a black comb out of my pocket and started talking about a stupid comb. The teacher, Miss Carlson gave me a B+ and told me it was a creative idea.

Whenever I saw Smokey's sister Pauline walking in the hallways of the school, I put my head down and kept my eyes on the carpeted hallway floor as I walked to my next class. I didn't like taking a bath and went to school with greasy hair. I didn't care about playing the clarinet anymore and would just pretend to play by moving my fingers. I wore the black snowmobile coat to school every day until spring arrived, when Paul sold the snowmobiles.

When I scheduled classes for my junior year, Bum talked me into dropping down to the comprehensive curriculum, which she said was much easier than business and college prep classes. Together we signed up for an electrician and shop class. The guidance counselor tried to talk us out of it, saying girls took home economics. We stood our ground and insisted that girls should be allowed to take shop classes. The guidance counselor had to talk to the administration and the administration had to take it to the school board. When we received our schedules the next school year we were delighted to see the electrician class on our schedule.

I'm not sure how I survived that year of my life as it felt like a blur. I put Smokey's death so far out of my mind, that it didn't surface until thirty-five years later when my husband Cliff and I were tapping maple syrup in the middle of winter. We used snowmobiles to get from one sugar bush to another. Cliff drove with me saddled behind him. When he came to a little hill, he slowed down. I could feel the sled bogging down in the snow and told him to hit the gas or we wouldn't make it over the hill. He wondered how I knew how to drive a snowmobile.

Memories of snowmobiling returned to my consciousness. It wasn't all at once, but more like the tip of an iceberg beginning to thaw. When I began writing my memoir and came to this time in my life, I included the snowmobile accident. I signed up for a writing class at Pitt-Bradford and submitted the chapter to the professor, Dr. Dani Weber. Dani had read some of my writing the previous year and we had a connection. As a child, she lived in Elgin, Illinois, which was about thirty miles north of Mooseheart. After reading the snowmobile story she brought it up at our next class, explaining what a tragic time it was for a teenager and that I needed to slow down and include more detail in the scene. The thought of writing in detail was agonizing to me, as I didn't feel as if I could remember anything else. I decided I would use my imagination to embellish the story.

While I was writing, I thought of a guy nicknamed Boogie, who was riding with us. His real name was Roger Young. I looked his name up in the phone and gave him a call to see if what I remembered really happened.

When he answered the phone I identified myself and told him about my writing assignment. I gave him a memory test by asking him if he remembered my brother's name. He clearly remembered each of them. I went on to ask him about the accident and he described it in detail just as I had written it. I thanked him for talking to me.

A few months later, I was at a wellness fair at the fire hall in Johnsonburg and I recognized, Smokey's sister sitting at a table. Gray short hair replaced the long brunette hair that she had as a teenager, but I still recognized her face. She was now a nurse and was handing out information on caring for the elderly. When no one else was at the table I mustered up the courage to talk to her. I nervously introduced myself, trying to look up more than at the floor and asked if she had a brother named Smokey. She said yes. I then asked if she felt uncomfortable talking about him as I knew he had died. She said not at all.

I continued to tell her that I was snowmobiling with him at the time of the accident and that we called him Smokey but I didn't know his real name. She told me it was Bobby and that she never talked to anyone who was there at the time of the accident. I told her how I felt it was my fault.

Shaking her head, she repeated the same words I heard her say at the funeral home, "Bobby died doing what he loved to do. He was a daredevil and said he was never going to live past twenty-one and he didn't." And then she added, "It wasn't your fault." My eyes began to water and the tears that welled up in my eye streamed down my face. I thanked her for talking to me.

The iceberg had now melted below sea level, but I didn't realize the full impact of the incident until a few years later when I started seeing a myofascial release therapist. She noticed my heart space was closed and did some body work to open it up. During our session, she suggested that I find more joy in my life.

That night I had a dream that I was driving a truck and was stuck in a snowbank with a snowmobile trailer behind me. I didn't know how to drive with a trailer attached to a vehicle so couldn't move forward or backward. When I woke the next morning, I thought about the dream and remembered that was the time in my life when I learned that having fun wasn't safe. The bottom of the iceberg thawed as I grieved all the years of lost joy and fun I missed in my life.

My heart welled with compassion for the young girl that went through such a tragic event in her life without any grief counseling to help her know that Smokey's death wasn't her fault.

Chapter Ten

During the summer of 1974, Gary and I went to the movies at the Diamond Theatre in St. Marys. We sat in the balcony of the elegantly decorated movie house, with beautiful chandeliers and burgundy velvet curtains, watching *Deliverance*, *American Graffiti* and other good movies. While watching a *Cheech and Chong* movie, Gary asked me if I ever got high. I was a little apprehensive to tell him the truth, but took the risk and told him yes.

He told me that he liked to get high once in a while. I told him about a cool head shop in Olean that Bum told me about. We drove up together and he bought me a red pipe and a gold marijuana leaf roach clip. As we drove back to his house to spend the evening, he warned me "Never say anything to mom about smoking pot or cigarettes. She doesn't like girls who smoke."

Gary's house was the perfect place to be whenever we were high and had the munchies. The cupboards were stocked with popcorn and snacks and there was ice cream in the freezer. My favorite snack was the home-made potato chips his dad made using a plastic slicer he purchased at the Clearfield County Fair. Bud dropped the paper-thin slices of potatoes into bubbling hot grease in an iron skillet until they were crispy brown. Then he drained them on brown paper grocery bags, put them in a bowl and salted them. Some of the slices would stick together and didn't get crispy. After making the potato chips his dad would head down to the PFL bar to drink the night away.

Christmas at Gary's house was a contrast from the artificial silver tinsel tree my mom put up in the living room of our apartment. The only other decorations at my house were fifths of whiskey and a large wicker laundry basket filled with fruit that my brother Bill gave my mom for Christmas.

After Thanksgiving, Gary's mom began baking Christmas cookies. Along with cut-out sugar cookies in the shapes of trees, bells and stars, she would make rosettes. Rosettes were made by dipping an iron shaped flower in a thin green and red batter and then into a skillet of hot bubbling oil where they swelled into thin, fragile cookies that were dipped in confectioner sugar after they cooled. The cookies were stored in round tins with Courier and Ives winter scenery on the lids for guests who would come treeing to the house during the holiday season. The nostalgic feeling of Christmas warmed my heart.

The decorated Christmas tree stood in the corner of the parlor. The parlor was a formal living room with a turquoise sectional sofa, with end tables adorned with starched doilies. The lamps on the end tables were decorated with a plastic garland in the shapes of candy canes, gingerbread, and sugar plums. A winter scene with fluffy white batting that resembled snow decorated the top of the Magnavox maple console television set. On Christmas Eve, beautifully wrapped gifts, which his mom had been gathering since sales began in October, were arranged underneath the Christmas tree with twinkling lights.

The family opened their gifts on Christmas morning and afterward stacked everything in neat piles. Relatives went "treeing" to each other's homes during the week between Christmas and New Year's Day. When guests came to visit, they would gather in the parlor and enjoy the tasty cookies and a glass of punch. Each of the family members would show the relatives what they received for Christmas that year.

Gary's family didn't go to church so there wasn't any mention of Christ in Christmas. And as much as I enjoyed the Norman Rockwell Christmas, I felt like an orphan who received a token gift compared to the large piles of gifts Gary and his sisters received. I felt sad and out of place not having gifts to give them in return. One of the gifts that I remember getting was a fake fur coat. I got the message that Gary's mom didn't like my bib overalls, flannel shirts, and blue jean jacket. I wore the coat a couple of times but it just wasn't my style.

After Christmas break, as my junior year was coming to an end, I was getting bored with the easy classes in the comprehensive curriculum. After I had dropped from Algebra II down to Math I, I had my fill of the redneck, beer drinking boys who were in the same classes and didn't care about learning. They were disruptive and rude. Bum and I excelled in the shop class, where we learned how to wire outlets and fix appliances but the redneck boys didn't like us in "their" shop classes and started calling us dopers.

During lunch, while we were walking down the middle aisle of the lunch room to empty our trays, Tim, a tall boy with blond hair that hung in his eyes and always had a wad of snuff stuffed in his bottom lip, began his ritual of calling us names. Bum and I walked over to him and his friend Sean Murphy, who was sitting next to him and threw our plates of half-eaten spaghetti at them.

Both Bum and I got detention; they got nothing although they did quit calling us names for a few weeks. It wasn't long before they were telling us to stick a needle in our eyes. Sean wasn't as big as Tim, so one day while he was walking down the hall, I went up to him and grabbed the collar of his shirt and shoved him up against the locker. Both Bum and I told him if he didn't stop calling us names he would end up dead somewhere and not to bother snitching because there was only one of him and two of us. He pretty much left us alone after that.

Whenever I went up to Gary's house, his mom talked a lot about having grandchildren. She was married ten years before she had Gary and was feeling left behind compared to her friends who were having grandchildren. She talked about how she loved sitting and rocking babies. For Valentine's Day, Gary gave me a pre-engagement ring with a little diamond on a gold band. I didn't realize I could have said no to a gift and didn't want to hurt his or his mom's feelings, but I wasn't sure I wanted to get married.

I started sending out applications for colleges and told Gary that I wanted to visit some colleges in the area. I felt a little defeated not having studied a language, but was determined to learn one during summer school. Gary had other plans for summer. Some of his friends, including my brothers, were planning a trip to Canada, and he invited me to go along. His cousin, Tom Uhl along with his girlfriend Ruth joined us, so I would have another girl to hang out with while the guys went fishing and drinking. We rented cabins in Northern Ontario where the guys brought home fish that we would fry up every night. Gary and I had our own bedroom where we slept together for a week.

Gary also started hanging out with a guy that was racing stock cars. On the weekends, we would go to the racetrack in Clearfield to watch the races. I found the experience extremely boring. The only thing I enjoyed were the salty French fries with vinegar. Repairing the race car in between the races began to take up a lot of Gary's time, and I didn't care for his obnoxious friend who was mouthy and rude, so I quit going with him.

One weekend when we were supposed to go to the races together, he called me and said he didn't love me anymore. There was another girl who he liked more. Her name was Mary Ann.

I was so hurt by the rejection but didn't let on. To get back at him, I went out on a date with one of his best friends that he worked with at Carbon City. Boy, when he got wind of that, he was livid. I started going downtown and hanging out on the Diamond in St. Marys, where it was easy to get an ounce of pot to get high. One weekend, I was sitting on a bench across from Ivan's men shop. Gary's dad drove around the diamond in his blue and white Cadillac. He recognized me and drove around the diamond again and pulled up to where I was sitting. He rolled down the window of the car and told me to get in. The car that reeked of King Edward cigar smoke.

"What do you want?" I asked.

"I'm taking you to the house. Gary is up there. You both need to work this out and stay together. Mona likes you and thinks you are one of the best girls Gary has dated."

We drove the few blocks up to the house and when I got out Gary came to the door with a red rose for me. His mom was standing at the door watching him. I didn't know what to say to any of them. I wanted to run away and tell them all to leave me alone, but the words wouldn't come out of my mouth. I was stuck and I knew it.

For my birthday that summer, Gary traded in the pre-engagement ring for a real diamond that included a wedding band for him and me. We would get married the summer after I graduated from high school.

Gary bought a 1960 red Volkswagon to drive around in the winter and bad weather to save wear and tear on the Torino. Together we rode on back roads and even though I didn't have my driver's permit, although I was seventeen years old now, he taught me how to drive the "bug."

I was determined to learn how to drive a standard. His mom didn't drive and had to depend on other people to take her where ever she wanted to go. My mom didn't drive a standard either. If my brother Bob's jeep was behind her car in the driveway of the house on Parade Street and he was sleeping, she couldn't go anywhere. My brother Warren got his permit and driver's license when he turned sixteen and wrecked Bob's new jeep, so no one bothered to teach me how to drive or asked if I wanted to learn.

I had taken notes on how to shift the gears in a standard, even doing it myself at times when Gary would engage the clutch on the Torino. At first, it took some doing, but I finally got the hang of letting off the gas, engaging the clutch and shifting the gears. I stalled the vehicle on more than one occasion. For some reason, Gary was patient with me whenever I was driving. I was never allowed to drive the Torino and I never asked about getting my driver's license.

In September of 1974, I went out to Southern Illinois with my mom and brothers for my brother Jack's wedding. Connie asked me to be a bridesmaid. I wore a sleeveless yellow summer gown and white hat with a large brim. Both she and Jack asked me if I would like to move to Illinois with them after I graduated from high school the next year. I said I would. When I scheduled classes for the senior year, I wanted to return to the college curriculum, but couldn't because I didn't have the necessary language classes. Instead, I signed up for the business curriculum.

Electric typewriters were brand new in the classrooms but first we had to learn on the manual ones. I didn't have enough strength in my little finger to push down the 'quote' and 'a' keys, so they were always a little faded. It was a challenge threading the typewriter with the ribbon that left my fingers black, but I learned to type fast and earned good grades. I also met new friends in the secretarial classes and the teachers, Mr. Berringer and Mr. Luther were kind.

I joined the Conservation Club, that was led by Mr. Clark. He taught us archery and how to tie fishing flies. What I enjoyed the most was going on field trips in the woods to cut brush for the deer.

The theme for the prom that year was *Time in a Bottle* from Jim Croce's hit song. I loved his deep voice and the folk melody. When I walked by the cafeteria where classmates were decorating for the prom, I wished I could participate, but didn't know how. No boy ever asked me to a dance and it never appealed to me to dress up in a gown.

My circle of friends was widening. I met a girl named Ginger who got pregnant while we were in eleventh grade. She gave birth to a little girl named Kelly and invited me to her apartment on Theresa Street. On weekends, she taught me how to make homemade bread using her grandma's recipe. The recipe specifically used cake yeast, which I had never seen before. She instructed me how to dissolve the yeast in tepid water and how to knead the bread.

I enjoyed holding her baby and rocking her to sleep while Ginger cleaned up the kitchen. Gary knew her husband Dave and we started hanging out together smoking pot and listening to Pink Floyd music while the baby was sleeping.

Another friend of mine, Theresa, also had a baby in eleventh grade. She married her boyfriend Mike and they lived in a little apartment above Stuart's Jewelry. Sometimes I would stop by and visit her after school for something to do. I was glad to have friends who weren't stealing and partying all the time.

My friend, Vicky, who was now out of school kept in touch. One day she called me up on the phone. "Hey Jeanette, I got a real job, other than babysitting, without a diploma. Can you believe it?" Mr. Newman, the English teacher failed her in his class and she was unable to graduate. It was drummed into our heads that kids without a diploma would never get a job.

"Wow, that's cool," I said

"Yeah, I'm working for a program called Planned Parenthood and I need people to go to a meeting. You can get free birth control."

Free birth control sounded pretty good to me. I was getting bored sitting at Gary's house watching TV on weekends. He didn't like spending money to go to the movies anymore. Also, I saw how much work babies were for Ginger and Theresa. They didn't have any free time to hang out with their friends. They had to stay home and take care of the babies while their husbands went out partying at night. That wasn't the life I wanted.

"Sure, I'll go with you."

"Cool. I'll pick you up next Wednesday after school around 5:00. The meeting starts at 6:00. She picked me up in an old red and black clunker that I was sure was going to break down along the way. The drive from St. Mary's to Ridgway was a little treacherous. The muffler of the car was held up by a coat hanger, scraping the road. My whole body was shivering in the icy January wind blowing into the car through the passenger window that was broke. Vicky lit up a Marlboro and handed it to me as we skidded around a curve.

I was relieved when we made it into Ridgway, passing the Mad Dog Saloon on the right-hand side of the road. We stopped at Vicky's apartment on Broad Street to pick up her sister Cookie. While climbing up the long flight of steps she whispered for me to be quiet so we didn't wake up the baby. The wood apartment door with a brass doorknob and chipped paint creaked as she opened it.

When we went into the apartment a beautiful girl with long brown hair and bright blue eyes, dressed in a muslin shirt was sitting in a bentwood rocking chair breastfeeding a little one-month-old baby girl. I had never seen anyone nursing a baby before and quickly looked away.

"Are you guys hungry? There are fish sticks in the freezer." Vicky said as she walked to the kitchen.

Following behind her I said, "I haven't eaten yet."

Vicky opened the 1950 style fridge that was completely bare except for a half of gallon of milk and an icebox full of frost. With a butter knife she started chipping away at the ice to free the box of fish sticks. In the meantime, Cookie had laid the baby down on a bare mattress on the floor. The babies' large blue eyes followed a sparkly Christmas ornament that hung from the ceiling.

"What's your baby's name?"

"Chelsea Rose."

"What a pretty name. It matches her rosy cheeks."

Cookie walked over to the gas stove and turned on a burner. She swept her long hair to one side and bent down to light a joint.

"Here, you want a hit, before we go to Vicky's meeting that she's dragging us to?"

Handing me the joint, I took a long drag. Vicky dumped the frozen fish sticks with a coating of white ice crystals on a blackened baking sheet and put them in the oven. We sat at the kitchen table and finished the joint.

"Hurry up and eat so we aren't late. This is my first meeting, and I have to get things set up." Vicky put a bottle of ketchup on the table. I tried to squeeze some ketchup out of the bottle, but the top was caked shut. While we were eating the nearly thawed fish sticks Vicky's boyfriend Nat, came into the apartment with his friends. They exchanged money for a bundle of pot. I began to get nervous thinking what would happen if they got caught dealing pot while I was there.

I stood up from the table and said: "I'm ready."

Cookie bundled up Chelsea Rose to go to the first Planned Parenthood meeting in Elk County. It was held in the upstairs of a two-story brick building on a side street in Ridgway. I was patient number 001 and Cookie was patient number 002. With the smell of pot and patchouli incense lingering on our tattered blue jeans and cotton tunics made in India, the two of us giggled and laughed as the nurse practitioner taught us how to do self-breast exams using a mannequin named Betsy Breast. I was examined by an old family physician with white hair and black rimmed glasses named Dr. Menteer. The clinic supplied me with a pack of birth control pills that I was to begin taking after my next period, which never came.

My next visit to the clinic was for a pregnancy test which was positive. I didn't feel like giggling and laughing at that appointment. The Planned Parenthood clinic referred me to an obstetrician named Dr. Lutz, who practiced in Ridgway. When I told Gary the news about the baby, I thought he would be mad but he was happy. He drove me to my first appointment, but wouldn't go inside with me.

The office was in the upstairs of a large two story white house in Ridgway. I was required to attend a 'childbirth class' where the nurse passed around vials of aborted fetus' at different stages of development. We were told that abortion was an option at this stage of pregnancy. I had never heard of abortion and wasn't about to kill a baby that visibly had a head, arms, and legs. The doctor told me I was too young to have a baby and that I didn't have any insurance to cover the cost. I was sobbing when I went out to the car.

"What's wrong?"

"The doctor told me I should get an abortion because I don't have insurance to pay for delivery and that I'm too young to have a baby."

"That's bullshit. Next time, tell him we will set up payments to pay for the delivery."

The next month I told the nurse, "I am going to have the baby and my boyfriend wants to set up a payment plan."

"Does he have a job?"

"Yes, he works at Carbon City full time."

"Well, the cost is about $500.00, if you don't need a Caesarean section."

"I'm going to have the baby naturally."

"We'll see about that."

Every month Gary gave me money to pay for the doctor visit.

When Gary and I told his mom that she was going to be a grand-mother, she was tickled pink. We also told her that he would be moving out of the house and that we would be living together. My friend Ginger had told me about a third-floor apartment where she was living at 745 Theresa Street for $200.00 a month, including utilities. It was a furnished one-bedroom apartment with small gas stove, a refrigerator from the 1950's and a black velvet over-stuffed chair and sofa. We shared a bathroom with an old man who lived across the hall.

The first thing Gary's mom asked was when we were getting married. We choose May 3 and she immediately began making plans for a wedding. We would be married at the United Methodist Church on North St. Marys Street. I chose my high school friend, Ginger for the maid of honor and Gary's mom chose Gary's sisters, Patty and Cindy as bridesmaids. I had a friend named Brenda at school who volunteered her mother, Mrs. Yale, to sew my wedding gown and the dresses for the bridal party which I would pay for with my babysitting money. I picked an empire style pattern for the dresses and a white cotton lace eyelet material for my dress. The wedding party dresses were made of purple, blue and yellow gingham with wide-brimmed straw hats to match. My dress had to be altered before the wedding due to my growing breasts.

Gary's best man was his friend Lee Dybowski, with my brother Bob and our friend Dick Snyder as groomsmen. Gary's second cousins, Renee Rung and Donny Rung were the flower girl and ring bearer. My brother Paul gave me away with prodding from Dottie. My brother Jack took pictures with a Nikon camera he bought when he was in Vietnam. My mom attended the wedding and wore a pink and white dress. I hadn't talked to her about being pregnant and although she knew, she was kind enough not to say anything.

A friend I knew from high school, Jodi Auman, sang the song *My Love* by Paul Mc Cartney and Wings at the ceremony. I wasn't sure how to feel about a wedding. I didn't like being dressed up in a wedding dress as it reminded me of the price I had to pay for the bride doll that 'Uncle Leo' had given me as a child.

As Gary and I walked down the aisle together and I saw my friends from high school as we left the church, I wondered what their future would be like. I resented their freedom and felt as if mine was lost. After the ceremony, when we came out of the church, the Torino was decorated with crepe paper and strung beer cans behind it. Gary was madder than hell because my high school friends used masking tape on his car.

The wedding reception was held at the upstairs of the Moose Club. The tables were decorated with white paper; brown Straub beer bottles wrapped in aluminum foil holding plastic flowers as centerpieces. Gary's dad paid for the booze and my mom made cabbage rolls, stuffed peppers and potato salad for the meal.

Gary and I went to Niagara Falls for our honeymoon. We stayed overnight in a hotel and went to the wax museum. We had to come back the next day because the clutch on his car was slipping. On the return home, we were stopped at customs. I had a joint and a pipe in the glove compartment so stashed it in a bag of garbage from Burger King. Customs rummaged through our luggage and searched the car. To our relief they didn't find the stash.

I graduated from high school in June of 1975. There were a lot of parties after graduation, but I didn't go to any as I didn't feel very good and knew that drinking wasn't good for the baby.

That summer my friend Vicky hitchhiked out west to live in a commune. Before she left, she told me that she was reading the Bible and wasn't going to be calling her dad, father anymore because the Bible said, 'not to call anyone your father, because your father is in the heavens.' She told me her dad became very angry and kicked her out of the house. The sadness I felt when she left was like a dark cloud that wouldn't go away.

To feel connected to Vicky, I started reading the old family Bible that I took from my mom's room when I moved out of the apartment on Parade Street. It was a black covered King James version with my sister Virginia's name engraved on the front. What I liked most about the Bible was that it had a list of all my siblings' names and birthdates, except for mine. I started reading the New Testament and particularly liked the words in red that were said to be the actual words of Jesus. I started praying the Lord's prayer at night before I went to sleep. It seemed to take away the fear I had about what it would be like to have a baby.

At the end of June, Ginger and her husband Dave invited us to see a Pink Floyd concert in Pittsburgh. They drove down with us in the Torino because their old car wouldn't make the trip. Gary parked the car quite a distance from the Three Rivers Stadium so it wouldn't get vandalized. As we crossed a bridge to the stadium, we walked over bodies lying on the concrete sidewalks, who were passed out on crystal meth. People were openly selling drugs.

When the band began playing *Money*, a crowd of over 46,000 people applauded. Everyone was smoking pot even with cops nearby. A girl named Cheryl from St. Marys passed me a pipe and I pretended to take a hit and gave it to the person sitting next to me. People began throwing sparklers and firecrackers that landed on people in the crowd. Although I enjoyed the music, I didn't like feeling unsafe. At the end of the concert, a huge black pyramid with a rainbow lifted in the sky.

Ginger and Dave invited us to stay at a friend's apartment in Pittsburgh where we stayed overnight. People were stoned and sleeping on the floors and sofas. A loud banging on the door woke us up in the morning. The cops came to bust someone.

Dave told us we had better leave so we grabbed our backpacks and headed home. It was a relief to leave the crowded city although the sweltering heat back at the third-floor apartment without air conditioning was intolerable. It was so hot that candles melted without me having to light them.

I didn't mind being alone when Gary was working second shift as I would go down and visit Ginger and play with her little girl Kelly. After she put her to bed I would go upstairs and just enjoy the peace and quiet. We didn't have money for a telephone line so no one called me nor did I have to hear my mom bitch or my brothers loud voices.

There was a room in the front of the apartment where I would iron Gary's clothes at night listening to the *Sergeant Pepper's Lonely Hearts Club Band* by the Beatles and *Moody Blues* albums. His mom had given me an ironing board and iron and taught me how to iron his jeans so there was a crease down the seams. I starched his work shirts and dress shirts and hung all the clothes including the jeans, on wire hangers. His underwear had to be neatly folded and socks all matched.

One Saturday morning, there was a knock on the door of our apartment. I was still wearing a cotton t-shirt that I wore as a nightgown. When I opened the door, there was a man dressed in a suit selling the *Watchtower* and *Awake* magazines. I gave him a dime for the journals. The knock at the door woke Gary up. He shuffled into the kitchen, wearing only his white Fruit of the Loom underwear.

"Who the hell was that?"

"A guy selling these magazines."

He picked up the journals laying on the table and tossed them in the trash can.

"Don't talk to those idiots again."

When I turned eighteen in August I was eligible to receive my share of the trust fund from the sale of the house and property that the government seized back in the 1960's. I had to return to Sharon to get the money and my mom had to be with me. Gary offered to drive us down in the Torino. My share of the trust turned out to be $1500 that we used to pay off the car.

Just like a bird building a nest, I spent the summer gathering items for the baby. Gary's mom had a baby shower and I received beautiful handmade afghans and brand new sleepers and diapers from relatives and friends.

While shopping with some of my "hippie" friends at the resale shop located on North St. Marys Street in St. Marys I spotted a ceramic feeding dish with compartments to separate the food. It had an opening to fill with hot water to keep the food warm. I thought about how nice it would be that the baby wouldn't have to eat cold oatmeal, like I did as a child. While I was looking at it, one of my friends told me he would pay for it as a gift. I accepted his offer.

While shopping at a mall, I came across a table with leaflets and books from the La Leche organization. I had never heard of the group, but I bought a small container of lanolin that they recommended for sore nipples when breast feeding. When I opened the container of lanolin, the earthy essence brought back memories of my Uncle Henry's sheep farm. When I returned home I read the stack of books and leaflets that were included in my purchase of lanolin. I ordered a Happy Baby Food grinder to make my own baby food from one of the catalogs. Along with my purchase I received a lot of information on natural childbirth and how to breast feed.

My sister-in-law Dottie gave me her copy of *Summerhill-A Radical Approach to Child Rearing* by A.S. Neil to read. I read the book cover to cover within days and wished I had been raised in a freeing environment. Idealistically, I hoped to parent the baby growing inside of me in a peaceful atmosphere of love and understanding.

Unfortunately, the mirror neurons in my brain of how I was raised were stronger than my ideals, and I would repeat some of the same modes of discipline and punishment that were inflicted on me onto my children.

Chapter Eleven

On November 6, 1975, I gave birth to a baby girl named Brandi Lyn Salter. We named her after the song *Brandy, You're a Fine Girl* by the Looking Glass. I expected the birth process to be a breeze, but it wasn't. The anesthesia made me sick, and I could barely walk afterwards. So much for a 'natural childbirth.' I wrapped her up in a cute sleeper and bundled her up in a pink, blue and yellow baby afghan one of Gary's aunts made for her. Car seats weren't required, so I held her in my arms as we drove home from the hospital.

Before we went home to the apartment, Gary said we had to take the baby up to his mom's house first. She had dinner for us, and everyone took turns holding the baby. When she started to get fussy, I told them I had to nurse her but his mom just kept holding her and wouldn't give her back.

"I think you should leave the baby here with me tonight."

"But I'm breastfeeding her."

"I have some formula and bottles here for her."

It was the first time I became angry with Gary's mom, and I felt guilty for being mad. I could feel my face becoming red and hot. I walked over, took the baby and wrapped her up in the afghan, left the house and began walking back to the apartment which was at least three miles away. When I got to the end of Mark Street, I heard the loud muffler on the Torino pull up beside me. When it stopped, I opened the door and got in.

I told Gary to tell his mom that this was my baby and that she had her babies and didn't say another word the rest of the way home.

When we returned to the apartment I layed Brandi in the white bassinet that was Gary's when he was a baby. Deep down I resented that he had things from when he was a baby and I barely had evidence that I was born.

I thought the baby would just go to sleep, but she didn't. She cried and cried. I didn't know what to do except sit and rock her all night. I was breastfeeding and didn't have any mentors or coaching. My nipples became so sore. I applied the lanolin from the La Leche League and it relieved the pain. I began to use it faithfully on any chapped skin and for diaper rash. The lanolin smell comforted me as it reminded me of smell of Uncle Henry's sheep.

When the snow began to fly the apartment was quite drafty. Gary's mom was worried how the baby would stay warm. The single pane windows had a thick coat of frost on the inside and the little gas heater barely warmed one room. We sat together shivering on the couch, hoping tomorrow would be warmer.

At Thanksgiving Dinner, Gary's parents told us there was a house for sale at 1169 Brusselles Street, a few houses up from where he grew up in the 1960's. It was a two-story wood frame row house with brown shingles and pink trim, right next to Gary's mom's best friends Vivian, and Joe Gabor. Gary's parent's had lived two houses up from the tavern at the end of the street when Gary was born in 1953. His mom talked at length about how much she missed the neighborhood on Brusselles Street.

Gary and I went to look at the house with his mom and dad. I bundled up Brandi in a pastel checkered snowsuit and a yellow insulated blanket. The house was old inside, but it felt like home. The entryway had old linoleum flooring that led straight to the dining room where there was a big wood dining room table with china cabinet and a buffet. I didn't have any china and wasn't sure what a buffet was for. Gary's mom pulled open the drawers with neatly folded tablecloths, napkins, and silverware and told me all the linens and furniture went with the house.

Next to the dining area, there was a small room with a couch, chair, end tables, and lamps; next to the dining area, there was a TV, couch, and a rocking chair. Gary said that it would make a great bar room. I wasn't sure why we needed a bar room in a house when there was one down the street. My feet were getting tired, so I sat down in the rocking chair and rocked Brandi back and forth with the sun shining through the windows. Gary's mom pulled the polyester floral drapes closed to block the sun from getting in the baby's eyes. I didn't know then how important light was to the soul and wished I could have told her to leave the drapes open.

At the back of the house, there was a small kitchen with a little kitchen table, an old refrigerator, and stove. A door in the dining room led to the basement of the house that had old empty Ball canning jars lined up on shelves wood shelving. In the corner stood an old wringer washer. It was just like the one I caught my hand in when I was four years old at Mooseheart while visiting my mom at Loyalty Hall on that Sunday afternoon. Suddenly, I felt like a little girl again. I felt as if my mom was in the next room hanging clothes on the line in the dank, dark cellar of the building that housed the mothers. I saw myself dragging a wood chair over to the washer and fishing out a red checkered apron to run it through the wringer. Except I forgot to let go of the apron I was holding with my left hand. The next thing I knew I was in the orphanage's dispensary with my left hand all bandaged up.

"Jeanette, Jeanette." I heard a voice say loudly. A ray of light flooded into the basement when Gary opened the storm door that led to the back-yard. I rubbed my eyes and wondered where I was at. I was alone in the basement. Jeanette didn't feel like my name. I felt more like Dorothy from the Wizard of Oz when the tornado came and the uncles took refuge in the storm cellar before the house was swept away by the storm. When I climbed the concrete steps to the outside, I wondered where the yellow brick road was. I thought maybe I would see my Uncle Henry, but the only person standing there was a stout man smoking a Kind Edward cigar who told me, "Mona took the baby over to see Vivian. What do you think of the house, Gary?"

I answered, "It's nice.

Then Gary asked, "Will you help me build a bar in the dining room?"

We told his parent's we didn't have a down payment for the house that cost $20,000. Gary's dad said he talked to my mom when he saw her at the Moose Club. She said she would lend us the 10% down payment and that the Italian guy who owned the house would sell it for $18,000. Gary agreed to pay my mom $50.00 a month until the down payment was paid off. By Christmas, the loan papers were filled out and signed. We went to the bank to get the money and keys to the house. Our house payment was $225.00 a month.

I packed up the baby clothes and our few items of clothing, including the black Bible that was on my nightstand next to the bed. We only had a few pots and pans and household items to pack. Gary put his stereo and speakers in the Torino, so they didn't get ruined. I put Brandi in the bassinet to nap while I lugged the few boxes down the three flight of steps.

Gary's friend Lee arrived with a truck he had borrowed from a friend. As usual, he arrived with a beer in his hand. His sandy colored hair was uncombed, looking like he just got out of bed. With a sheepish grin that redeemed his obnoxiousness he asked,

"Hey, what needs to be done?"

Gary replied, "The Christmas tree needs to be taken down."

Lee looked out the third story window and said, "The truck is right down there, so we won't have to haul it down all those f…ing steps."

He grabbed the artificial Christmas tree with a couple of little dough ornaments I had made from salt and flour and drug it into the kitchen, opened the frosted window and threw it outside. Green, red, and gold glass ornaments shattered on the sidewalk.

There was a bar of Ivory soap on the sink, and I wanted to take it and shove it in his mouth. I was beginning not to like Lee. He worked third shift at Sylvania and stayed up all night. On the weekends, he and Gary went out all night drinking and driving their race cars around town. Gary would come stumbling up the apartment steps drunk as a skunk and sleep all day.

This didn't change when we moved into our new house. In fact, it got worse. The Three Son's Tavern, was less than a block from the house. Gary spent quite a bit of time there after working at night. When he left, he didn't lock the front door of the house. One night I woke up to hear someone coming up the steps hollering Gary's name. I grabbed a loaded pistol that was in the nightstand beside the bed and went to the top of steps and pointed it right at the guy's head. He held his hands up and said "Whooaaaa. I'm Gary's cousin, Tommy Salter."

With both of my hands holding the pistol steady, I said, "I don't care who the hell you are. Get out of my house." He turned around and left. The door was always locked after that incident.

It wasn't long before money became a problem. After Gary was paid from Carbon City every two weeks, he would give me $50.00 for groceries and said he would pay the rest of the bills, except he didn't. Overdue electric and water bills started to arrive in the mail. I became anxious and wondered how I would survive without utilities. My mom wasn't getting paid. The phone would ring at two o' clock in the morning with her on the end of line, hollering at me that she wanted her money back. I felt like I was drowning without a life jacket or lifeguards to pull me out of the water.

I did the only thing I knew how to do and started screaming at Gary to get the bills paid. I tried to save money on the electric bill by washing the clothes in the wringer washer instead of going to the laundromat. I was proud of myself for not getting my hand stuck in the wringer. On warm, sunny days, I would hang Brandi's diapers outside on the clothesline to dry. Gary still wanted all his clothes pressed and soft, so we would haul the wet clothes to the laundromat to use the dryer.

When I was outside hanging clothes, Vivian the next-door neighbor would wave and say hello to me. I waved back, but I never knew what to talk to her about. She asked me if I was going to grow anything in the garden. I didn't have any idea how to garden but told her we were going to plant some bean seeds that I found in the shed out back. I used an old hoe and dug a trench to plant the seeds. The only things that came up were weeds and grass. Gary mowed the back yard with the old push mower Mr. Catalone had left at the house.

One day, Gary came home with a little white puppy that we named Casper. He had no idea how to house train a dog so that was left up to me. I wasn't much better and screamed at the dog when it went to the bathroom in the house. It never did get fully potty trained. We should have never gotten a dog. I felt like I was carrying this huge load of bricks already and someone just added another one to the pile.

In the Spring, Gary's mom started questioning me about when I was going have Brandi baptized. I told her I hadn't thought about it. She insisted we get her baptized at the same church where we were married and called the minister to set things up. All this was very confusing to me; Gary's mom didn't attend church but yet wanted the baby baptized. When I asked her about it, she said Brandi needed to be baptized to wash away original sin. If babies died and weren't baptized they wouldn't go to heaven. Now I was totally confused. At the meeting, I asked the young minister how a baby could sin when it didn't even know right from wrong. He skirted around the issue and told me that baptism is a way of welcoming the baby into the Christian community. That made more sense to me so we went ahead with a small informal baptism. Our friends, Ginger and Dave Johnston were supposed to be the godparents but never showed up.

I started making homemade baby food from the Happy Baby Food Mill grinder from the La Leche League and tried my best to feed Brandi healthy food. Dr. Roman Babin was the only pediatrician in town so I took her to him and he recommended a book by Dr. Benjamin Spock on *Babies and Child Care*. The book became my Bible. I read it day and night and it answered many of my questions about caring for babies. I enjoyed being a mom and taking care of Brandi. She started sleeping all night and was a quiet, content baby during the day.

I wasn't prepared for a baby getting sick though. When Brandi was five months old she spiked a high fever so I took her to Dr. Babin. The fever was so high that he hospitalized her immediately. Her room was in isolation because of the unknown origin of the fever. I was able to stay overnight with her because I was breast feeding. After all the tests came back negative, Dr. Babin said they were going to do a spinal tap. The procedure scared me and I prayed so hard to God that he would make her well. It was the first time I prayed since Smokey was killed in the snowmobile accident. The next day a rash broke out all over her little body and she was diagnosed with the roseola virus. I was relieved and thankful to God.

Over the winter, my friend Vicky moved back from the commune and was now living on Mill Street in St. Marys. When Spring arrived, I strapped Brandi to my back using a green backpack I had ordered from the La Leche League and rode into town on my bicycle to visit Vicky and her boyfriend, Nat. Vicky now had a baby, Hannah, who was born at the beginning of June. I guess the Planned Parenthood didn't work for her either.

Vicky taught me how to make her mom's Italian Zucchini Soup with hamburger, tomatoes, corn and of course, zucchini. It was the first time I had ever tasted the summer squash and liked it. Vicky also introduced me to tacos. No one in this area had heard of the Mexican meal. Vicky said they ate a lot of them when she was at the commune in New Mexico. The hard corn shells were just coming out in the grocery stores on the East Coast. They were tasty and easy to fix.

On one of my visits, John and Mary Jo Crana, an elderly couple dressed in business clothes were discussing the Bible with Vicky. After they left, Vicky told me they were Jehovah's Witness and she was studying the Bible with them. I remembered what Gary said about not talking to them. I didn't want to lose Vicky as a friend so told her that was okay but Gary didn't want me talking to them.

Vicky was just setting up housekeeping and told me about the Jewel Tea man that stopped at her apartment to sell her household items; if I bought things from him, she would make money. I told her I would give her money to tell him not to come to my house.

A natural foods store opened less than a block from Vicky's apartment. She told me about a natural chocolate called carob that they used at the commune to make marijuana brownies. When we went to the store to get the brownie mix, I bought a book, *Let's Have Healthy Children* by Adelle Davis. While reading the book, I felt conflicted because I smoked cigarettes and knew it wasn't healthy. Instead of quitting smoking, I gave up the idea of eating healthy.

By the end of summer, the money situation at home was getting worse. I couldn't figure it out. Gary had money to go out drinking on the weekends but didn't have money for the bills. He told his dad that we were having problems paying the bills and tried to borrow money from him. His dad was the supervisor at Carbon City where Gary and my brothers worked. Gary brought home a job application and told me I could start working the next week.

When I told Vicky that I was going to work at Carbon City, she took a long hit of a joint and told me I wouldn't like it. She had worked there one day, and my father-in-law told her to hit the road. But off to factory work I went, working second shift driving back and forth to work with Gary while his mom and sister Patty took care of Brandi. I learned to run presses and had to fill the hoppers with carbon graphite powder that was dirty. The powder was a fine dust that clung to my clothes and shoes. I had to use Fel's

Naptha soap to remove the black grime from my hands, that became rough and chapped.

Gary was a die-setter and taught me how to use a micrometer to measure the parts. I began running two or three presses at a time and worked my way up to picking parts off the press before a shoe came and pushed them off and damaged the part. I often became bored with the job and would do senseless stuff, like putting a paintbrush under the press to see what would happen. Unconsciously, I was trying to get fired from the job, but that didn't work. Gary would just scream and start throwing parts when the press needed to be adjusted or finally broke down.

Out of the blue, while running a press, picking off hot parts and lining them up on trays, I came to the realization that I was making parts for chairs, automobiles and other machinery. I told myself that I was making parts to contribute to people's well-being. That realization made the work tolerable.

The girls at the plant were rough. They swore and went out drinking after work. To fit in, I started to pick up their habits. They didn't smoke pot, but they sure could drink. After work on Friday nights, they would stop at the house to drink at the bar that Gary's dad built. We always left the baby up with his mom to stay overnight so we could sleep in the next morning.

Just as Vickie said, I didn't like the factory work; I lasted eight months. While picking parts off one of the presses, a punch came down and clipped the top of my finger off. Gary's dad was the supervisor and had to take me to the hospital to get it bandaged up. I had the week off and enjoyed the time off work, staying home and playing with Brandi. I told Gary I wouldn't be going back to work at the factory.

Gary wouldn't give me money for groceries and the bills weren't getting paid again, and I knew I needed to find a job. I told Gary I wanted to get my driver's permit so I could get a job to help pay the bills. He took me to the driver's center in Ridgway and I passed the test for the permit.

"You'll never be able to drive the Torino though."

I informed him "If I can't drive the Torino, then I'm not going to get my driver's license and then I won't get a job. Plus, the Torino isn't good for a baby. She's getting too big to sit on my lap. I can't put her in the middle because of the shifter, and we can't use the back seat because of the speakers."

He agreed to sell the Torino. We traded it in for a Yellow Opal Cadet, which was smaller, but had four doors. And it was a standard. I worked at getting my driver's license and after a few tries passed the test. I found a job advertised in the Daily Press for a bartender at the Elk's Club in Ridgway. I filled out a job application and within a week received a phone call from Leo Parisi, the manager. He wanted me to come to Ridgway to talk to him. Leo was a short Italian man that smoked a pipe. The first thing he said to me was "I see on your job application that you were at Mooseheart. Why do want this job?"

"Because I need the money."

"Have you ever bartended before?"

"No."

"Good, I can teach you how to do it right then."

"Can you start this weekend? The other girl quit. I pay five dollars an hour, under the table and the tips are good."

I started that weekend and Gary's mom was more than happy to have Brandi stay overnight while I worked and Gary went out drinking.

The Elks was a high-end bar, and I learned how to pour a shot without using a shot glass and how to pour a glass of beer with a perfect head. I learned how to make Manhattans, Martinis, Whiskey Sours and my favorite Kahlua and Cream. After getting home at 5:00 am a few times, I learned how to get a bar cleared out at closing time. Even though I was eighteen, I started drinking behind the bar for free. The local judge frequented the club and after drinking a fifth of Scotch, left a fifty-dollar bill on the bar. When he returned a few months later, I gave him back the money. He told me it was a tip. One day he noticed a burn on my arm and asked if my husband was abusing me. I told him the truth, that I burnt it on the pizza oven. He told me if my husband was hurting me to let him know and he would take care of it.

With good tips, I was now making enough money to pay the electric and water bill. But things weren't so good at home. I was feeling lost and lonely in life, so I started praying to God. Lo and behold, one day a Jehovah's Witness lady with an eight-year old little girl showed up at my door at about ten o clock in the morning. She introduced herself and her daughter. Mary Lou was a tall, slender woman with a kind smile. Her young daughter Pammy had blonde hair with bangs and was wearing a dress holding the Watchtower and Awake journals. I invited her into the house and she complimented me on how nice my house looked and asked me how I felt about the prospects of a nuclear war. I told her I was frightened for the future of my little girl. The Vietnam war had ended, but I was terrified of a nuclear war.

She told me that the earth wouldn't be destroyed by nuclear annihilation, but it would be transformed into a beautiful paradise where my children and I could live forever. She opened a green hardcover Bible to Revelation 21:3 & 4 and read about a time when there would be no more tears or crying, and death would be no more. Then she flipped to another scripture in the book of Isaiah and read about how the lion and lamb would live in peace together, and about children playing upon the aperture of a snake. I was impressed with how well she knew the Bible.

Mary Lou explained that this generation was the one that was living at the time God's Kingdom was set up in the heavens in 1914. In 1977 "this generation" was in their eighties. The time of the end would come within ten years, twenty at the most. I swallowed everything she said hook, line, and sinker. She offered me a little blue book with gold embossed letters, entitled *The Truth That Leads to Eternal Life* for the cost of a dollar. I recognized the book from Vicky's house.

She asked if I had a Bible. I told her I had one upstairs. Brandi had crawled up on her lap and seemed content, so I quietly climbed the wood steps, trying not to wake Gary. The tattered black bible was in the top of the drawer. As I was leaving the room, I noticed Gary starting to move. I hoped I didn't wake him. When I returned downstairs with the Bible, Brandi was playing with Pammy on the green living room carpet. Mary Lou showed me a scripture from John 17:3. She asked me to read it aloud. I read, "You will know the truth, and the truth will set you free."

And then she asked, "Would you like to have a free home Bible study to learn more about God's word?"

I didn't think twice. I wanted to know more about the Bible.

"Yes."

I thought her jaw was going to drop to the floor. I would find out later, that not many people accepted their offer of a Bible Study. We set up a time for her to visit the next week. Along with the book she left me a copy of the Watchtower and Awake journals for ten cents each.

After she left I thought that perhaps this was the freedom I was looking for but didn't find after getting out of Mooseheart. Perhaps now I would be free of my fears about raising my daughter, free from my family and free from the loneliness I felt inside.

After she left, Gary came downstairs. "Who the hell was here?"

"A lady who knows Vicky. I'm going to have free Bible Study with her."

"I told you before not to talk to them."

Before Mary Lou left she warned me that people would not like me talking to Jehovah's Witnesses, but that was Satan trying to prevent me from learning about God. I believed her and was determined not to let Gary stop me from learning the 'truth.'

Mary Lou started bringing two single women called 'sisters' to the house with her for the weekly Bible studies. Sue and Annette were 'pioneers' and spent over sixty hours a month in the field service. Mary Lou was a single mom with three children and didn't have money for gas to travel from Ridgway to St. Marys every week so turned the Bible study over to the pioneers. Also, she said studying with me would help them 'get their time in.' I didn't realize it at the time, but I was slowly being indoctrinated into the religion by learning all the new terms that weren't familiar to people who weren't Jehovah's Witnesses.

Each visit, they brought me current issues of the Watchtower and Awake. I read the journals cover to cover. I hadn't read anything of value since graduating from high school and it was interesting to be learning new things that were happening all over the world. I began looking up scriptures in the old family King James Version of the Bible. I tried to read the Bible a few times by starting at the beginning but always became bored after the story of the flood.

During our Bible Study, the sisters encouraged me to read from the green hard covered New World Translation of the Bible. They explained that the name Jehovah was taken out of the majority of Bibles and that I should use one that restored his name. The fact that their Bible was in modern English made it easier for me to understand, so I put away my old Bible. I arranged for the 'sisters' to come earlier in the morning when Gary was sleeping. Sometimes he would hear us talking in the downstairs and would ask me who was there. When I told him Jehovah's Witnesses, he would roll his eyes.

The first few chapters of the book *The Truth That Leads to Eternal Life* warned that Satan would use family members and friends to stop me from gaining eternal life by criticizing my decision to study the Bible with Jehovah's Witnesses. True to their word, when I told people I was studying the Bible with Jehovah's Witnesses, they would say negative things. When I told my older sister, who was living in Connecticut at the time, she told me to never talk to her about Jehovah's Witnesses. We weren't close growing up, and I didn't know what I was going to talk to her about now. The only person that didn't oppose or try to stop me from studying with Jehovah's

Witnesses was Gary's mom. She had friends who stood for her at her wedding who were Jehovah's Witnesses.

The sisters invited me to go to a meeting at Kingdom Hall on Sunday. They didn't use the word church. I hadn't been to a Sunday service since I left Mooseheart. Gary had been at the Wizard bar until four a.m. so I got up early, ate a piece of toast and dressed in my faded blue jeans, a yellow halter top, and Dr. Scholl's blue sandals to attend the meeting.

The ladies at the Kingdom Hall all wore dresses and the men wore suits and ties. Even though I was dressed differently, everyone came up and said hello and introduced themselves. No one paid that much attention to me in my whole life.

I expected to hear some of the old hymns such as *The Old Rugged Cross* and *Jesus Loves Me* but that wasn't the case. At the beginning of the service they sang an unfamiliar song, said a prayer, and then a man gave a sermon for nearly an hour. Then they sang another song and for the next hour studied the Watchtower magazine by reading paragraphs and answering questions. It was long and boring, but the people there were so nice to me.

The bartending job at the Elk's Club was beginning to cause a conflict for me. Vicky's sister Cookie lived in Ridgway and would come to the bar in the evenings while I was working. She was also studying the Bible with Jehovah's Witness. Men would buy her drinks and we would get into discussions about the Bible. I started bringing my green Bible to work to show the men that we were living in the last days; the attention they gave Cookie came to an abrupt end and so did our discussions.

At home, Gary started talking about wanting to have another baby. His mom was enjoying Brandi, but she wanted to have a grandson. I was feeling conflicted with bartending and having another baby seemed to be the solution. Being pregnant gave me a reason to quit bartending without Gary getting upset that we didn't have enough money. He promised to start paying the bills and give me money for groceries every two weeks.

On Friday's I began visiting with Gary's mom after her husband went to work. She didn't drive so I would take her shopping, and we would go to eat together. At one outing as we were eating a fish fry at a little restaurant on the Million Dollar Highway she confided in me that she had started bleeding again and would be going to the doctor for a pap smear. She was a little nervous because she hadn't been to the doctor in twenty years since she gave birth to her youngest daughter Patty.

His mom had just turned fifty and I didn't know anything about menopause and didn't think anything of it. When the results of the pap smear came back postive she had a hysterectomy. After the surgery, the doctor informed Gary's dad that his wife had cancer. He instructed the doctor not to tell her she had cancer. But when the biopsy reports came back there wasn't a choice but to tell her as she required chemotherapy and radiation. She went through the treatment at the Andrew Kaul Memorial Hospital. I wasn't allowed to visit her at the hospital because I was pregnant. I felt so sad and confused. My mom's boyfriend Fred had died of cancer, but he smoked cigarettes. Gary's mom didn't smoke, or drink and I didn't understand how she could get cancer. After the treatment Gary's dad assured everyone that she was cancer-free.

Gary was happy to get me away from the bartending, but he couldn't get me to stop my Bible Studies with the Jehovah's Witnesses. As I became more involved, I learned that if I wanted to qualify for everlasting life, I had to stop celebrating pagan holidays and birthdays. This didn't seem like such a big deal since my family didn't do much to celebrate holidays. If I loved God and wanted to learn more about him I would also have to attend meetings on Tuesdays and Thursdays at the Kingdom Hall. At the meetings I met more 'friends' and for the first time in my life, I had a sense of belonging.

At the meetings, I met a woman named Judy who had two elementary aged girls named Beth and Vicky, and a baby named Jonathon. Judy was also expecting a baby about the same time as my baby was due. Before and after the meetings Beth and Vicky would play with Brandi. She loved the attention they gave her. Judy invited me over to her house in Ridgway for coffee when her husband wasn't home. David was a chiropractor and didn't like her being a Jehovah's Witness.

While I was visiting Judy, she told me she delivered her babies at home with the help of her husband. She went on to explain that David was an 'unbeliever' but she was in subjection to him, except about spiritual matters. He made it hard for her to get to the meetings and if her older son Eric didn't want to go to meetings he didn't have to.

When I went home, I told Gary that I would like to have a home-birth but he was adamant and said no. Judy encouraged me to read about the Lamaze method of childbirth that I could use in the hospital. A new OB/GYN, Dr. Lin, had just moved to St. Marys so I made an appointment with him. When I asked him about the Lamaze method of childbirth he told me there were classes at the library. Since Gary worked second shift I attended the classes by myself and learned how to breathe and what to expect at the birth. I was again introduced to the La Leche League to help me with nursing.

The more I was around Jehovah's Witnesses, the more I wanted to fit in. Smoking cigarettes and pot were against Jehovah's will, so that meant I would have to quit the habits. I cut back smoking pot when a high school friend was blowing marijuana smoke in her two-year-old daughter's face to get her high. The little girl began to have seizures and I wondered if it was from all the pot smoke. I didn't feel comfortable smoking around the children and didn't like worrying about getting busted so it wasn't too hard to quit.

Kicking the cigarette habit was another story. Vicky and her sister Cookie had quit smoking and were to be baptized at the 1976 convention in Pittsburgh, Pennsylvania. They urged me to join them, but I couldn't kick the habit of daily smoking two packs of Marlboros. I needed to start going door to door to warn people about the time of the end or else I would be blood guilty, but I couldn't go out in service unless I quit smoking. I put God to the test and prayed harder than I had when I wanted to get out of the orphanage. Each time I craved a cigarette, I would pray and eat a candy Lifesaver. It was hard with Gary smoking all the time in the house. After not having a cigarette for a day I would rummage in the ashtray for a butt and would light it up and smoke just enough to make me feel light headed and sick. After the birth of my son on May 20, 1978, I finally kicked the habit.

I wanted to name the baby Josiah, but Gary didn't like the untraditional name and really didn't like it when I told him it was from the Bible. I didn't have any other names in mind so Gary's mom helped me name him. She said she always like the name Justine, but since he was a boy I named him Justin Lee, the middle name after Gary's friend.

A day after the baby was born and he was circumcised, the nurse brought him to me for nursing time. He was sobbing uncontrollably, and she said I could keep him with me for as long as needed. My heart broke when he continued to sob through the nursing. I had no idea how cruel the circumcision procedure was.

A month before I had Justin, Judy gave birth to a little boy named Andy. The 'sisters' at the Kingdom Hall had a baby shower for the two of us and gave me clothes for a little boy. Everyone was so nice to me.

When Justin was a few months old he began crying a lot and wouldn't nurse. When I took him to Dr. Babin, the pediatrician, he told me he had thrush and needed to be hospitalized. I stayed at the hospital and nursed him while he was given nystatin. When the infection cleared up and we came home, Judy called to see how the baby was doing. I told her about this thing called thrush; she told me it was a yeast infection and that I should give him yogurt.

I tasted yogurt once at Vicky's house, and it didn't care for it. Judy encouraged me to give him a teaspoon at a time and that it would be better for him than the medicine. She gave me a copy of *The Yeast Connection* by William Crook to read. I learned that the yeast infection probably came from me taking birth control pills and drinking too much alcohol. I absorbed as much of Judy's advice as I could.

Judy told me about a food co-op called Genesee Natural Food where I could buy bulk natural foods inexpensively. We split ten pound bags of raisins, flour, spices, whole grain pasta, cheese and gallon buckets of peanut butter. I bought a Blue Ball Book and taught myself to can food, using the empty canning jars in the basement. I became interested in making healthy food but went a little overboard. Brandi, who was now three years old, had a hard time adapting to the texture of whole grain bread and pastas. When I brought home a dozen of brown eggs, she said "Oh no, whole wheat eggs!"

Soon, I became accustomed to attending meetings at the local Kingdom Hall three times a week equaling five hours a week. We traded in the black and yellow Opal for a blue and white four-wheel drive Bronco and Gary bought a second car, so I would have a car in case something happened to the kids while he was working. I started driving myself to the meetings.

There was always one more thing I needed to do to please Jehovah and the next thing was to go door to door at least two times a week, equaling at least ten hours and sometimes up to twenty hours a week. The well-organized door to door work with maps of Elk County broken down into small areas was called 'field service.' We kept good records of each door in the 'territory' and persistently went back to each door until we found someone home. I mail ordered a leather book bag made by Jehovah's Witnesses to hold my Bible, magazines and books to offer to interested people. I was coached at the meetings on what to say and how to reply to people's objections.

I didn't feel shy about knocking at people's doors except when a man would answer. When I went out 'in service' with Judy, she told me just to imagine them getting out of bed and putting their pants on just like everyone else. Other than that I was excited to share the 'good news' with people and tell them about the paradise earth.

The Watchtower Bible and Tract Society had answers for everything. If we ever had a question we were instructed to look up the answers in bound volumes of Watchtower and Awake magazines dating back to the 1930's. I didn't have to think for myself. This felt familiar because as a child I was raised with rules and regulations for everything. My clothes were chosen for me, meals were chosen for me, a whistle blew to wake me up in the morning, to eat in the afternoon, for supper, and to go to bed at night.

In addition to all the meetings every week and field service, I now was encouraged to attend two-weekend circuit assemblies in the spring and the fall and a five-day convention in the summer that were held in Buffalo and Pittsburgh. Gary didn't want me to drive out of the area to large cities and refused to let me take the car. I traveled with a single sister who helped me with the kids. I helped with directions and learned how to read a map and navigate around large cities.

The conventions became our family vacation time and the children looked forward to staying overnight at a motel. I took the children shopping and bought each of them a new toy to compensate for not having Christmas. When conventions were in Niagara Falls I was able to take them to see the falls. Traveling and overnight accommodations were a big chunk out of our meager budget which didn't make Gary happy. I justified the expense by all the money he spent on cigarettes and beer.

On September 23, 1979, I was baptized at a circuit assembly in Olean, NY. I was told that this date was the most important day of my life; even more important than my date of birth and that I should always remember it. I felt privileged to be one of God's elect.

Christmas came that year without me buying presents for the children or helping decorate a tree. Gary began spending more and more time at the bar and I spent more and more time with my new family, Jehovah's Witnesses.

Out of the blue, I received a phone call from my brother-in-law who lived in Connecticut. He called to tell me that my sister had a nervous breakdown and wanted to see me. I felt bad for her and told Gary I would like to go out to visit her. Although I had never flown before, I called a travel agency to find out that a plane ticket would cost one hundred dollars. We had two hundred dollars in the bank. I was surprised when Gary said I could go. Gary's mom was delighted to have Brandi stay with her for a week. Justin was still nursing, so I took him with me.

When I arrived in Connecticut, my brother-in-law picked me up at the airport in a beat up old car. The house they lived in wasn't clean. My sister was out of the hospital and if she was happy to see me, I didn't know it. She screamed and hollered at the kids and made fun of her youngest daughter Tammy for talking so much, calling her motor mouth. The phone rang off the hook with bill collectors calling to be paid. I tried to tell my sister about my studies with Jehovah's Witnesses thinking it would give her some hope, but she adamantly reminded me to never talk about that religion around her. I didn't know what else to talk to her about. When I returned home and Gary told me about all the parties he went to while I was gone, I understood why he didn't mind that I spent the money to go see my sister.

I began to realize that marrying Gary was a mistake, and I wanted out of the relationship, but the Bible didn't allow for *a divorcing*, except for adultery. Gary didn't like the responsibility of marriage and told his parents that he wanted to move back home with them. They told him that he had a family to take care of. We were both stuck in the relationship. Gary was also getting tired of people at work asking about me being a Jehovah's Witness. They told him to tell me not to be knocking on their doors.

Gary applied for a job at the Coor's plant out in Golden, Colorado. I thought perhaps it might be a good move for us and when he was offered an interview we flew out together for a week with our infant son Justin. Brandi again stayed with his mom for the week.

I fell in love with the mountains and sang John Denver songs for months. We put our house up for sale, but it didn't sell. During the same time period, his mom was diagnosed with stomach cancer. We took the house off the market and decided to stay put.

On June 15th, 1978, my ninety-six year old Oma passed away from colon cancer. With my two little children in tow, I attended a funeral service for her in Sharon. Instead of feeling like I was with family, I felt as if I was with a group of strangers. She had a rose in her hand for her one, great, great, grandchild. I wished she had a rose in her hand for me. I thought about the little girl, Rose I created in Mooseheart and didn't feel any emotion.

The only other person I knew who had cancer, was my mom's seventy-five year old boyfriend Fred, who had died a few years earlier. My mom took me to visit him once when he was in the hospital. Gary's mom was only fifty three years old. Gary and I drove to Danville to see his mom after she had surgery to remove cancer from her stomach. When we returned home his dad told us that the doctor closed her back up after the surgery because the cancer was so bad. When she returned home, she lost weight rapidly and after two years of suffering, she passed away on January 9th, 1981. Before she died, I told her about the resurrection to the paradise earth and how we would see each other again.

Having a son meant a lot to Gary, and he tried a little harder to be a better father. We began going camping together, although he still liked to go out drinking after work. After he got into a brawl with my brother Bill at the Three Sons Tavern and came home with a black eye, he quit going out at night. I was happy until a new bar, The Wizard, opened up at the end of Brusselles Street only a mile from our house. Gary informed me he got a job as a bouncer that he was getting paid for. I never saw any of the money.

Unable to process the grief of Gary's mom having cancer and with no coping skills to deal with the stress of Gary's drinking, I began having excruciating headaches that would cause me to lay in bed for days at a time.

I found myself screaming at Brandi and Justin for the simplest things, such as not picking up their toys. I didn't realize I was supposed to teach them how to clean up after themselves. I thought children just automatically knew how to do things. I resorted to spanking when they didn't comply. I tried taking Excedrin, but the caffeine kept me up at night. I tried to eliminate all artificial ingredients from my diet, to no avail.

Chapter Twelve

Although money was tight, we were able to get a personal loan to pay my mother back the down-payment money she lent us for the house. I thought the random phone calls in the early morning hours would end, but they didn't. My mom spent a lot of time at the Moose Club where she met another boyfriend. Her mental illness was taking a toll, not only on me, but on my sister-in-law Dottie. After coming home from a day of drinking at the Moose, she barged into Dottie's house unannounced and was leaving dirty laundry piled up in the basement.

Dottie couldn't take it anymore so her and Paul sold the house on Parade Street to Gary's cousin, Tom Uhl. Some of the guys that Paul worked with started up a new powdered metal factory in Michigan and invited him to go along, so him and Dottie moved as far away from my mom as they could get.

My brother Bill bought a house on Rightmeyer Street where he and my mom lived. She bought a piece of land near the East Branch Dam for my brothers Bill, Bob and Warren to build a camp. She always had a pipe dream of owning a log cabin and this was her last chance. Instead of a log cabin she got a camp made from salvaged barn wood on three acres of swampy land.

My brother Jack moved to Pennsylvania from southern Illinois, with his wife Connie and their little boy Matthew who was six months younger than Brandi. They moved in the upstairs apartment on Parade Street. Jack got a job at Carbon City. Connie and I got along well. She was a Christian and asked me about the Jehovah's Witnesses. I invited her to a meeting and she went with me one time. Although the religion wasn't for her we still got together so Brandi and Matthew could play. Jack and Connie didn't stay in St. Marys very long before they moved back to Illinois.

Gary and I started camping together with the two children. With our income tax we bought a tent, and sleeping bags. On weekends we enjoyed camping at the East Branch Dam, Loleta State Park, Beaver Meadows and any place we could find with a swimming area for the kids to play in the water and sand. For the first time I started to feel like we were a real family and we were doing something we all enjoyed.

My friend Vicky started a business selling Tupperware products and I helped her out by having parties at my house. She soon went to the top of the ladder and earned a new car and trips to Florida. For one of the events she needed a special dress made and asked me to sew it for her. I needed some extra help making it so Marcia McClintock, one of the 'sisters' offered to help me. She invited me to her house on Gardner Hill in Weedville. I didn't have anyone to watch the kids so I took Brandi and Justin with me and they played with her kids while we sewed.

On the way home, as I was going down the hill on a freshly oiled and graveled road another car was coming. When I swerved to miss the oncoming vehicle, I overturned the steering wheel of the four-wheel drive Bronco and the vehicle skidded, rolled over and landed in a cornfield. When I turned around to check on the kids I expected to find one of them dead or seriously hurt. It was miraculous that they were both okay. We crawled out of the vehicle and sat in the cornfield and said a prayer to Jehovah, thanking him for protecting us and keeping us safe. Even though we were in the middle of nowhere a man in a van came by and stopped to help us. He had a box of doughnuts and offered one to the kids and then gave us a ride down to Mary Lou's house located in Byrnedale. When we arrived at her house, I felt something warm on my leg and looked down to see blood oozing from my thigh.

I was so afraid to call Gary to tell him what happened. He was often angry when I spent time with the 'friends' out in service. And this wasn't the first predicament involving Jehovah's Witnesses. He was still resentful that I took Brandi and Justin out in service with Mary Lou, in a car that barely ran. It was late spring and we were out on back roads with five children in the car 'looking for Jehovah's sheep' on backroads still covered with snow. Mary Lou's car got stuck in the heavy wet snow. The children and I spent at least three hours in the car without food or drink while she walked out of the woods for help.

Thankfully when I told Gary about the accident he was happy that none of us were hurt. He came down and got us and took me to the hospital to get stitches in my leg. When he saw how bad the Bronco was wrecked he couldn't believe we weren't hurt. When the vehicle rolled over most of the glass from the windows shattered outward instead of inside, protecting us from harm. I was in a state of shock for a few days and had to get a new pair of glasses, but all in all I was thankful to God for our safety. I was determined more than ever to do anything He wanted.

Brandi started kindergarten at the Spruce Street School in St. Marys. I was instructed by Jehovah's Witnesses to talk to her teacher to explain that Brandi wouldn't be saying the Pledge of Allegiance or celebrating holidays or her birthday. I didn't realize how much stress this would put upon a child. When I told her teacher, Mrs. Masson, about the restrictions, she looked deeply concerned and sad but did her best not to make Brandi feel excluded by paying extra attention to her.

Not only was I making decisions that would affect my daughter's social skills, I was indoctrinated to make a life or death decision as to whether my children or myself would receive a blood transfusion if we ever needed it. When I decided to be a Jehovah's Witness, I agreed that if it came down to needing a blood transfusion or dying, we would die, believing that we would be resurrected to the paradise earth. I was also teaching my children that Armageddon could come any day and took away their hope and dreams for a future life. The Watchtower Bible and Tract Society's books, including books printed for children, contained graphic pictures of people who weren't Jehovah's Witnesses being destroyed at Armageddon. This included their daddy, grandparents and other relatives.

A woman named Joyce, who lived on Bucktail Road, started attending the meetings at the Kingdom Hall. We started riding back and forth to meetings and assemblies together. I was embarrassed to learn that her husband, Stan, was the high-school principal when I participated in the walk out. I hoped he wouldn't tell her what a bad egg I was. Stan had retired from teaching and now owned a real estate business. Joyce had five children; only her two younger boys Jeff and Joel attended the meetings with her. When I met Joyce, I felt as if I had a friend for life. We both had unbelieving husbands and she was easy going and relaxed. In between the hours she spent helping Stan with the real estate business, we went out in service together traveling many miles of back roads to spread the 'good news of the God's kingdom.'

Gary was still getting flack from guys at work about me being a Jehovah's Witness, as I was knocking on their doors. I wanted to be a pioneer, but couldn't swing the ninety-hour requirement, so I signed up every month as an auxiliary pioneer where I spent sixty hours a month preaching. Gary decided to apply for a job at GKN Sintered Metals in Emporium where he had lived for four years when he was in high school. At the time his dad worked at a powdered metal factory in Austin.

I had been to Emporium a few times when we were dating and took rides to visit his friends Ronny Mack and Denny Shoup. We always stopped to say hi to 'Mom and Dad Shoup' who lived in a stone farm house on the edge of the town. We had attended their twenty-fifth anniversary celebration when I was pregnant with Brandi. They were a kind couple who were grateful to Gary for getting their son Denny to high school every day.

When Gary got the job at GKN, I was now expecting my third child. We put the house on the market and it sold right away. I took that as a sign from Jehovah that we were doing the right thing. I knew some of Jehovah's Witnesses that lived in Emporium from Circuit Assemblies and contacted them to help me find a place to live. We ended up with a little apartment on Fifth Street owned by George Coppersmith. Emporium was not only geographically isolated from nearby towns, but I would soon learn it was also socially isolated.

On moving day, we loaded up a U-Haul with our furniture and household belongings. Along with dozens of boxes, I had packed enough emotional baggage to fill a boxcar that would take me years to unpack. Driving a red Zephyr station wagon with Brandi in the front seat, I followed the moving truck that Gary was driving down the long hill of Goetz' Summit. Justin was excited to be in the front seat of the U-Haul truck. As we passed the roadside rest at the bottom of the summit and crossed a railroad track, it became difficult for me to breathe. I felt as if I was moving to the last track on the railroad. Even though I had put my childhood out of my conscious mind, I felt like the Red Caboose at Mooseheart that was on the lone railroad track. I had again, shut out where I came from and again, had no idea where I was going in life.

Epilogue 2012

Valerie stayed with Cliff and I for two short months that seemed like an eternity. While staying with us, she cleaned every nook and cranny of my house until it shined like the top of the Chrysler building, rearranging furniture, pictures, the silverware drawer and anything else that she thought was out of place. Her incessant talking took a toll on our quiet lifestyle. Lilly and Valerie stayed up late and slept in the next morning. Lilly missed the school bus on more than one occasion and when I tried to help out with time management suggestions, Valerie became defensive.

Before Valerie and Lilly came to live with us, a friend asked me what I would do if she had an alcohol problem and things didn't work out; plan B was CAPSEA, a woman's shelter in Ridgway. Some friends that I knew from the Episcopal Church were looking for someone to help with housekeeping, and I was able to get Valerie some part-time work, but the first item on her shopping list when she got paid was wine from the liquor store. It was time for Plan B.

I made an appointment with a counselor at the shelter to see if they had an opening. I talked Valerie into moving downtown where she would be closer to her work, shopping and the library. Valerie was an avid reader and read more books in a month than I could in a year. With a little wrangling her and Lilly were able to get into the shelter, but that didn't last long. There were too many rules. Valerie and I learned at Mooseheart that rules were made to be broken. Within a month, Valerie was kicked out of the shelter for not respecting the curfew. Somehow, she landed on her feet and ended up cleaning a high-end Bed and Breakfast, where the proprietors let her stay in a carriage house behind the business. Lilly made friends with classmates that lived in town and seemed happy. I invited Valerie to have Thanksgiving Dinner with us and forewarned my kids of her incessant talking. I didn't think of how lonely and out of place Valerie would feel with all of my kids and grandkids here. She commented more than once on how lucky I was to have a family.

With Christmas right around the corner, Valerie was able to get her eighteen-year old daughter, Emily, to fly from out west for the holiday. Valerie and I drove to the State College airport to pick Emily up, but we arrived an hour late. Emily was quite upset with her mom for not being on time. Valerie arranged for Emily to stay in the elegant B&B that was decorated beautifully for Christmas. She gathered gifts for both girls through the social service agencies and on Christmas morning they had a fairytale Christmas, with everything except snow.

Valerie intended that Emily would fall in love with Pennsylvania and stay here, but Emily would have none of it. Her ticket was round trip. I sensed there was friction between the two of them and found out why when Cliff and I drove Emily back to the airport; she shared with me that there were five bottles of wine on the tab when it came time to pay the bill with her step-dad's credit card.

Out of the blue, Emily asked "How do you know my mom?"

"We were in Mooseheart together."

"What is Mooseheart?"

"Your mom didn't tell you about our childhood in an orphanage?"

Emily's eyes widened in surprise and she shook her head no.

I wanted Emily to understand her mom's background so I told her about the time I was forced to spend hours in a dark basement copying scriptures from the Bible because I didn't change from my street shoes into my slippers when I came in the house.

As I was telling her the story, Emily became short of breath and asked me to roll down the window. I asked if she was alright. She confided that her mom never told her about Mooseheart and then asked me why I was normal compared to her mom.

As we were nearing the airport, I didn't have enough time to tell her what it took for me to get to where I was. I could only tell her it was due to many years of counseling and by God's grace.

Valerie and Lilly stayed a month in the carriage house before they were evicted to make room for the annual chainsaw carvers that would be coming to town in a month. Valerie told Lilly they would be moving back to our farm, which got back to me through my granddaughter Paige. I felt as if I was in the wading pool with my head just above water, but this time I wasn't going to let Valerie push my head under. Cliff and I both made it clear to her that she wouldn't be moving back to our house. Valerie agreed to make an appointment with a mental health counselor and looked around for an apartment, but without adequate references and steady income things didn't work out for her.

The only alternative was for her to go back to California. She booked a train trip back with only a suitcase of clothes. It was disappointing for Lilly to leave all the new toys she received for Christmas behind. The ride back to the Pittsburgh train station was quiet, with Lilly in the back-seat coloring and Valerie staring out the window with tears streaming down her cheeks. Before she boarded the train, I gave her a gift bag with activities for Lilly and a letter explaining how sorry I was that things didn't work out.

I felt as if we were being separated again, just as we were at Mooseheart, but this time I was able to say good-bye and wish her well. She thanked me for all I did and promised to repay me some day.

I hope she does repay me someday. Not with money, but with a phone call telling me that she took care of herself and that everything in life worked out for her. I hope she found a job she was able to keep and a home she was able to clean and rearrange. And most of all, a counselor, like Dr. Francis, who helped me untangle all the knots of my life.

As for me, when Valerie left Ridgway, it was as if a thousand-pound weight was lifted from my heart. She did call a few weeks later and said she was going to return as soon as school was out. When I answered the phone and heard her voice, I felt as if I couldn't breathe. With my voice shaking, I told her a three-day train trip back to Pennsylvania wouldn't be fair to Lilly. I was crushed at the thought of turning her away and had to call Dr. Francis to regain my footing. He assured me that it wouldn't be a good thing for her to return and that I had done the right thing.

Although I felt sorrow for her and Lilly I had a renewed sense of appreciation for the obstacles I overcame and a deep appreciation for my community and family that bestow me with a sense of belonging and love.

Valerie and I never talked about God and that saddened me, as I know I wouldn't be where I'm at today without His guidance and presence in my life. After I moved to Emporium, feeling like a red caboose stuck on the railroad track, my true journey with God began. I unearthed memories and emotions buried deep within myself, but was led out of the isolating darkness and loneliness that threatened to destroy me, into a life of true happiness, love and meaning.

Acknowledgements

———•———————————•———

My deepest appreciation and love to my husband Cliff for believing in my story and encouraging me to write. I'll always remember the support you gave me by selling your road bike, so I could follow my dream and travel to Manzanita Beach, Oregon for a writing workshop. Thank you for your unending love.

To my four children, Brandi, Justin, Cherey, and Caleb, thank you for the love each of you bring to my life. I didn't expect that when I had children, I would have loyal, loving and trustworthy companions in life.

To my grandchildren, William, Jeremy, Paige, Emily, Ariana and Camdyn, you fill my heart with love and my life with purpose and meaning. I love each of you to the moon and back.

To my brother Jack, I'm grateful I wasn't alone on my journey and am thankful to have a big brother that I look up to and respect. To my other siblings whom I'm not so close to, I know you all care in your own way and I'm sorry that things haven't worked out for the best between us.

From my community, I thank my friends Kathleen Lawrie, Barb Miller and Mary Dunton McGrath for believing in me and helping with the book. To my dear friend, Dr. Ray Francis, thank you for helping me untie the knots in my life, so I could tell my story in a coherent manner. My deepest appreciation goes to my dear friend Mary Lisa Gustafson, for your editing expertise and unconditional friendship.

I was blessed with great writing teachers including, Lisa Lepovetsky, Nancy McCabe, Dr. Dani Weber and Jennifer Lauck. Each of you inspired and challenged me to develop the craft of writing and encouraged me to tell my story.

My greatest thanks to God, for keeping me safe and for your guiding light in the darkest of times.